THE SECRET THAMES

A BIRD'S-EYE VIEW OF BRITAIN'S MOST FAMOUS RIVER

Photographs by SKYSCAN

Text by Duncan Mackay

In association with the

TED SMART

To our children, Robin and Abigail

A TED SMART Publication
This edition published in 1993
by arrangement with Ebury Press
an imprint of the Random Century Group
Random Century House
20 Vauxhall Bridge Road
London SW1V 2SA

Editor: Jane Struthers
Design: Behram Kapadia
Map: Helen Holroyd

A catalogue record for this book is available
from the British Library

ISBN 0 09 182474 5

Typeset in Palatino by Textype Typesetters
Printed and bound in Italy by
New Interlitho S.p.a., Milan

Contents

Foreword

This book will help us all to know the River Thames even better, and I am delighted that the Countryside Commission was able to support the initiative. I particularly commend the separate chapters because the Thames is so varied. We all have our favourite bits. I confess to a special liking for the stretch from Oxford to Godstow and Swinford Bridge which gives the ideal short walk. But it is the Chiltern Thames which is my own. The Goring Gap, where the river squeezes between the Berkshire Downs and the Chiltern Hills, is high drama in the landscape. On a clear day, I look at it from the Oxford plain as a great gateway.

But the Thames is everyone's river. It cuts a swathe across southern England. It is part of the nation's heritage: redolent with history – from the dreaming spires of Oxford to the royal buildings of Hampton Court, the Tower of London, and Greenwich – and celebrated in our art and literature.

The river has long been an important thoroughfare, linking settlements along its route. Crossed by fords and ferries, now marked only by place names, and by ancient routes such as the Ridgeway, it was a focus for trade and activity. It is fitting that a National Trail should follow its course.

The Thames Path, which the Countryside Commission is creating, will run from the river's source in Gloucestershire to the Thames Barrier in London. It is due to be officially opened in 1994, when four new footbridges will have been built over the river, the towpath and river banks repaired, new sections of footpath created, stiles and gates erected, and the complete route waymarked.

The Thames Path is expected to be England's most popular National Trail. Many people live nearby, and access to the route is easy by public transport, car, bicycle or boat. Above all, it is level and low lying, so there is no need for special clothes or equipment. Everyone can enjoy it, from small children to the elderly, whether they walk it in part or from end to end.

This book reveals secret delights that the Thames has in store if, like myself, you enjoy savouring the pleasures that England's countryside so freely offers and learning about its history and customs.

Sir John Johnson
Chairman, Countryside Commission

Introduction

Through time's quirky flow the Thames has run for perhaps a million years. Thousands of deeds (fair and foul), hundreds of kings and queens (ditto) and the waxing and waning of fortune have made the river truly worthy of John Burns' poetic description of it as 'liquid history'. Throughout that history, the Thames has seen many bizarre incidents, and in this book I have tried to uncover some of the secrets that lie along the banks of this famed river.

The emphasis in this book is on the whole Thames Valley – on the unusual, the over-looked, the bizarre, and some of the situations through which the Thames Path will wind. The text and photography are just lures, fishermen's flies, sprats to catch mackerels, for out there is the real thing and it cannot be experienced second-hand. Whether by foot, boat, punt, bicycle, train, plane or balloon, this book intends to tempt you to sample the many charms of the Thames. Once a highway, a border, barrier, water supply, laundry, power tool, factory, fishery and lavatory, the river also links history, culture and national, tribal fortunes together in a swirling mix as strong as any weir pool eddy.

The simple pleasure of being able to walk alongside and experience the river from source to sea will soon be available to everyone when the Thames Path, the Countryside Commission's only National Trail to follow a riverbank route, opens in the mid-1990s. It is the Thames path that forms the golden thread through this book, weaving people, incidents and landscape with the weft and warp of time and place.

To guide us, the landform and geology have broken the length of the Thames into convenient chunks: from the oolitic Cotswolds, through the clay vale of Oxford, uprisen chalky Chilterns, the outwashed gravel terraces with their royal palaces, to the tide-scoured alluvium of the estuary mouth.

It is for you to travel your own path, but if this book plants a few seeds along the way then it will have nourished a greater understanding of a remarkable river valley which is truly a special place worthy of special care.

DUNCAN MACKAY
December 1991

The Work of Skyscan

We use a novel system for aerial photography based on balloon-borne cameras. A 26ft (8m) long balloon is tethered to a Land Rover to carry a remotely controlled camera platform into the air. This platform has both a TV and a stills camera mounted on it, arranged to have exactly the same field of view. The TV picture is displayed on a monitor in the Land Rover. With this viewfinder system we can control the aerial platform to compose the photographs precisely without having to leave the ground ourselves.

Compared to other aircraft, the absence of vibration and stability of the platform produce sharp, clear photographs with superb depth of colour. The balloon can be flown close to buildings, and the height is easily varied from 6 to 600 feet (1.8-180 m). It does not suffer from the same restrictions which apply to powered aircraft and it can be flown anywhere in the country, as the photographs taken in London of Big Ben and the Monument illustrate.

There is no environmental disturbance caused by the balloon's operation, as no energy is consumed in staying aloft and it is completely silent in flight. The balloon is inflated with helium, an inert and safe gas. This is recovered using a compressor for subsequent re-use, helping conserve a finite natural resource.

In effect we have married the eighteenth century invention of the balloon with the twentieth century technology of electronics and photography. This unique photographic journey along the Thames reveals the countryside in stunning detail. This, together with the interesting and informative text, will, we hope, generate even more appreciation of this historic river.

Acknowledgements

There are many people we ought to thank for helping us to produce this book and if there are omissions due to lack of space, their contributions were nonetheless appreciated. Our thanks go firstly to Carol Rees of the Countryside Commission and Fiona MacIntyre of Ebury Press for making the project possible. Thanks also to Duncan Mackay for providing a fascinating text to accompany our photographs, one which clearly demonstrates his depth of knowledge of the Thames Valley and the new Thames Path. His quest to find hidden aspects of the river led him to walk many a Thameside mile, knowing that the thirst generated by his endeavours could be refreshed in the numerous pleasant hostelries along the way.

Grateful thanks go to the many landowners who freely gave us permission to fly a balloon from their properties; the personnel of the Civil Aviation Authority for their efficiency; and the Cardiff Met. Office for accurately interpreting the seaweed.

Our family deserves a special mention, both to our parents for their unswerving support and to our children Robin and Abby for their forbearance whilst we devoted time to photography whenever the weather permitted.

Andy and Brenda Marks

SKYSCAN
AERIAL PHOTOGRAPHY
AERIAL ADVERTISING

The Thames Path

The creation of the Thames Path by the Countryside Commission as a new National Trail has been the stimulus for this book. By the end of the century the whole route should be open to the public, leaving all but London's most intractable urban sections to follow suit. The Thames Path is unique among the family of National Trails because it is the only one to follow the entire course of a single river. When completed it will be 290 km (180 miles) long and add to the existing 2697 km (1676 miles) of National Trails already open to the public. It will cost approximately £1.2 million to create and involve the erection of four new major pedestrian bridges.

National Trails were originally called Long Distance Routes, but their name was changed to reflect their significance to the nation as pathways along which extensive journeys can be made in peace to admire the best and most characteristic landscapes in England and Wales. The Thames Path, which is crossed by the Ridgeway, already a National Trail of some repute, is an example of a growing number of walking, cycling and horse-riding routes throughout the countryside. The Ridgeway, which coaelesces with the Thames Path at Goring, has been described as the 'oldest road' and is looked upon as an ancient channel for human and animal movements over the chalk downlands. The Thames has also served the same function as a highway for an equally long time.

The birth of the Thames Path

The idea of a walk alongside the Thames from source to sea was first suggested in 1926 by the then Council for the Preservation of Rural England. The Thames Conservancy played a strong hand, having been in control of the river as far as Cricklade since 1866. Riparian owners and local authorities were also generally sympathetic and walkers' organizations, led by the Ramblers' Association, brought attention to the route's potential.

The source of the Thames, Coates, Gloucestershire

Enveloped in the protective branches of the Thames Head ash tree this plain stone marker indicates the source of the mighty River Thames. Formerly the site of a gushing spring it is now bone dry in all seasons. It is the start (or finish) of the Countryside Commission's latest National Trail, the Thames Path, which is the only long-distance walking route to follow the banks of a single river from its source to the sea.

After the Second World War there was a sharp decline in the barge traffic delivering goods from the Midlands to London via the canal system, and the towpath fell into complete commercial disuse. It was already in terminal decline because of the expansion of the railway system, although the east coast threat to shipping posed by German submarines during the war had given the Thames a brief burst of renewed business life as a safer route into London for war materials.

Along with a return to peace came a call for greater public access rights to the countryside, and in 1949 the National Parks and Access to the Countryside Act was passed, giving rise to the Peak District National Park and the Pennine Way (the first Long Distance Path to be created, in 1951). The Countryside Act of 1968 created the Countryside Commission and its programme of policies for the promotion and protection of the countryside. Although the Thames Path had always been considered worthy of recognition, some of the classic Long Distance Routes, as they were then known, were given priority for implementation. Voluntary bodies such as the Ramblers' Association, however, kept up a steady pressure to have the Thames Path officially designated as a Long Distance Route. The Association produced its own booklet showing how it could be done, in large part using existing rights of way, and an official proposal from the Countryside Commission was finally approved by the Secretary of State in 1989.

One legacy of the former commercial use of the river, the towing path which forms the basis for the Thames Path downstream from Lechlade, was its ferry system. Horse ferries were used to transfer the towing horse from one bank to the other, often where landowners refused permission for the towing path to enter their land or, in some cases, to avoid natural obstacles. This produced a pattern of public rights of way which switched from bank to bank as the horse-drawn barges were towed towards London. When the commercial barge traffic died so did the horse ferries, thereby marooning great stretches of public highway often without landward ingress or egress on the bank. This was a real obstacle to the plan to produce a continuous Thames Path and is why the final product contains proposals to create at least four new bridges and frequently uses lock gates and weirs to cross the unfordable river.

The creation of the Thames Path is a dynamic project involving dozens of individual local authority staff and teams within the regional office of the Countryside Commission in London and the National Rivers Authority in Reading. For the first time, sponsorship will play a direct role in harnessing the interest of the business community in the creation of a National Trail. It is appropriate that one of the world's greatest rivers has been chosen to lead the way in this manner into the next century. It will be a project to delight millions of visitors and local people alike.

The Lyd Well, Kemble, Gloucestershire

The keen, low sunlight of early spring in the Cotswolds Area of Outstanding Natural Beauty warms the trees surrounding the Lyd Well. In summer and some dry winters there is very little water to be seen here, but occasionally the spring is very forceful and justifies its name of 'lyd' (loud) as it gurgles and bubbles noisily to the surface. West of this site, the infant Thames frequently runs dry all the way to the source. The Thames Path follows the curving wall on the left.

Cotswold Thames

The Thames, which is known as a mighty name in riverine folklore, begins its journey to the sea in the parish of Coates, in a place as dry as a twig. It was not always so and our ancestors knew the magic of this secret place and the mysterious birth of the river they called 'the dark waters'. The fledgling Thames skirts Celtic Kemble and is ignored by Saxon Cricklade, or perhaps it is just warily watched because this river floods, suddenly, over the wide silty wastes whenever snow melts. All around, the stamp of the land is Cotswold: the predominance of creamy stonework, lichen-spattered stone slates, the ash trees on the village greens, the kingcups by the water's edge, the summer sounds of sheep and harvest. The upstanding scarp that makes the Cotswold Hills an Area of Outstanding Natural Beauty dips gently here with less drama but retaining the unique Cotswold harmony of vernacular style and mood. Through this warm landscape the Thames Path winds on its exuberant course, a mirror to the youthful stream. In many places a new route will have to be created in places where rights of way are absent and the tread of man has long since given way to mechanized agriculture. Possibly because of all this gentility, the Cotswolds survives as a real place as it enfolds people in its mildly eccentric charm. Further downstream, as the Thames slides east past Inglesham and Lechlade, so the Cotswolds slip away like the Cheshire Cat until, by Radcot Bridge, only the fondness of its smile remains.

There is a secret at the heart of the source of the Thames which history has not passed down to us with clarity. Does any one single place deserve to be called the source? Certainly many people consider the 'official' source of the River Thames and the beginning (or end) of the Thames Path to be near Trewsbury Mead, but there are also the swampy lands within the boundary of 12 ancient markers in the parish of Aewylme (Ewen) which lay claim to the title. In Colwich near Cheltenham the Seven Springs perpetually rise to flow down the River Churn and give lengthier credence to their geological permanence as an alternative source. The Ordnance Survey and the Countryside Commission, however, are unequivocal about the matter and locate the source squarely on the map in Trewsbury Mead. Although

Somerford Keynes, Gloucestershire

Glorious mirrors to the azure sky, the water-filled lagoons of excavated gravel pits near Somerford Keynes threaten to inundate the stripling Thames. The Thames winds a barely wet and woebegone channel between its big blue brothers; it shares this isthmus with the Thames Path. The lines of trees and hedges that stretch like spiders' legs through the water either mark the boundaries of former fields or have grown around the network of footpaths and bridleways.

there is not a drop of water anywhere, there is an ash tree on which the letters 'TH' (for Thames Head) could once be seen. Above it are the banks of the Thames and Severn Canal, now as dry as the source of the fabled river itself.

Here was once Wolu Crundel, the cleft mark in the ground at the head of the Thames. In Roman times and later, as early engravings would have us believe, this now dry spring shot pressurized water into the air like a fountain. The Iron Age Celts from Trewsbury Fort would have regarded this place as sacred and offered sacrifices to its water divinities. Earlier still, it may have been marked by the Hore Stone, or Athelstan's Stone, which is no longer to be seen. Now only a plain slab marks this historic spot.

Eastwards, downstream across the meadow, the embankment of the A433 now hides the course of the Roman road, the Foss Way, which runs from Cirencester to Bath. Over the road the banks of the disused canal and the remains of its old pump house lie half hidden. In 1792 it was a scene of action, with a Boulton and Watt beam engine pumping water from the oolitic aquifer below to replenish the canal. Between the A429 and the A433 there is a spring, marked by a wind pump, which nearly always produces water. This is the Lyd Well (loud well) which in winter still bubbles noisily. To the south-west is Kemble, which derives its name from that of a Celtic god, and to the south-east is Ewen (Aewylme), which means 'great spring'.

Here we step into another slowly unfolding mystery of the secret Thames. Diligent research suggests that hereabouts was an area of land granted by King Athelstan to the Abbey of Malmesbury in 931 in the Saxon Charter of Aewylme. The charter mentions 12 significant ancient geographical or stone markers subscribing a water meadow of 5 hides – 243 hectares (600 acres) – called Yeoing (ewe-ing) Field, on which 3000 ewes were grazed. This land is swampy because the underlying aquifers are faulted, and so water either oozes to the surface as mud or shoots up as springs. Perhaps Mother Isis is to be found here; not a river in its own right but the collective expression for many springs which give birth to the Thames.

The 'stripling Thames', as English poet and critic Matthew Arnold poetically called the river, runs slowly between Ewen and the two villages of Ashton Keynes and Somerford Keynes. At Ashton Keynes a delightful Cotswold village blends harmoniously with the stream bed, comforted by green strips of roadside grass and crossed by many little bridges. In Somerford Keynes there is an old Cotswold manor that still retains the close association of church and manor house. Both villages are linked by the word Keynes, a derivative of de Kaineto, the name of a Norman landlord from the eleventh century.

The landscape hereabouts is colourfully decorated with fields of cereals and rape seed. Coots and moorhens paddle through the unassuming river to call attention to its watery focus. Between Ashton and Somerford Keynes, however, an abrupt change occurs which significantly alters the Thames from a river in a wide developing valley to a channel that runs through an immense blue landscape of massive gravel-extracted lagoons. This alteration in the riverscape is startling and even the course of the Thames becomes confused between the Keynsian villages, being replaced for a while by the more aggressively channelled (and less attractively named) Swill Brook. The Thames Path finds a way that is agreeable to everyone through this dramatic blue landscape.

Nar Mead and Cricklade

Two disused canals, the North Wiltshire Canal and the Thames and Severn Canal, used to cross each other just west of North Meadow at Cricklade but are now water-filled hollows in the landscape and a spawning ground for frogs.

The ancient Nar Mead, as the North Meadow is known locally, is a splendid remnant of the once vast commons, open fields and Lammas lands of England. It is not only a relict agrarian institution but also one of the last habitats of the snakeshead fritillary and rare water meadow flowers such as the once ubiquitous yellow rattle. North Meadow is so vital a habitat that its 45 hectares (112 acres) have been declared a National Nature Reserve by English Nature. It is old church Lammas land and is grazed by right-holders only between 12 August and 12 February, but English Nature now owns most of these ancient rights. Such a perpetual regime of management has preserved the millions of fritillaries that grow here and the exuberant abundance of other flora. Plough it once and all this would be lost, as so much has been all along the Thames Valley. The fritillaries bloom briefly for a few weeks between March and April when the ground is still wet but are swiftly destroyed by visitors who do not keep to the footpaths.

The right of upstream navigation on the river ends at Cricklade, which has always been an important crossing point of the Thames. The town was once a frontier post between the Saxon kingdoms of Mercia and Wessex. King Alfred passed through with his army in 878 and King Cnut (Canute) repeated the event in 1016. The river also meets its main rival in the battle of the sources here; the River Churn (the longest tributary of the Thames) flows down strong and hearty from its permanently bubbling spring at Seven Springs, near Cheltenham. Cricklade has a splendid cruciform church (St Sampson), the lesser known St Mary's closer to the river and a plank bridge where baptisms by complete immersion were performed in the Thames during the nineteenth century.

Hidden between Cricklade and Castle Eaton are the remains of Eysey Chapel and part of the river called Cow Neck. Castle Eaton has a counterpart in Water Eaton, where the River Ray enters the Thames, but of the castle itself there is no clue. The Thames Path cuts away from the river here and avoids Kempsford, which is a pity, although its massive tower – erected in the fourteenth century by Henry, Duke of Lancaster – is impossible to ignore.

Cotswold industries

It can be hard to reconcile the pastoral nature of Kempsford's past, when the great water meadow in the bend below the village was full of sheep (more than 5000 in Elizabethan times), with the twentieth-century presence of RAF Fairford to the north. Perhaps it was easier to imagine the roars of battle between the Hwiccians and the Wessex Saxons who fought here in 800 whenever a flight of USAF B-52 bombers took off during the 1990–1 Gulf War. Kempsford is a splendid village and one cannot fail to be impressed by the powers of the canal builders who managed to squeeze the Thames and Severn Canal between the church and the village.

Kempsford, like many places in the Cotswold Thames, retains significant reminders of the wealth and influence of agriculture as an economic activity. The size and artistry of the churches certainly reflect the endowments given by successful sheep farmers in the medieval and later periods. The bountiful combination of good grazings on lush riverside meadows and the power of the stream for washing and fulling the wool was a double blessing. The fact that much of the landscape was also underlain by Fuller's Earth (the principal ingredient for fulling) simply added to the natural advantage of the location. Sheep farming was the wealth provider that made the Cotswolds the place it is today. It also had a significant impact on the River Thames as a trade route and the development of London as a mercantile base from which fortunes were made in exporting wool. The real Dick Whittington made his money in wool and his fame as Lord Mayor of London. Even today the woolsacks in the House of Lords remind us of the power that came to the nation from the backs of Cotswold sheep.

The Thames and Severn Canal

Lying past a bend in the river, Inglesham has two buildings of importance hidden away: its Round House and its church, St John the Baptist's, which is splendidly restored to a delightfully simple form. William Morris, the nineteenth-century poet and craftsman, directed the work for the Society for the Protection of Ancient Buildings, an organization which he helped to found in 1877.

Inglesham Round House is one of five lock-keeper's cottages that belong to the drama of the construction of the Thames and Severn Canal. It is round like a lighthouse after the unusual, but economic, style established by its designers in the 1780s. Horses were stabled on the ground floor and people lived above, with a flat lead roof to act as a water tank. Here at Inglesham the Round House marks the grand entrance of the canal into the Thames.

The Thames and Severn Canal was a massive engineering undertaking, the Channel Tunnel of its age, and the realization of a peculiarly British dream to forge a continuous transport link between east and west at a time when roads were generally impassable for heavy traffic. Anyone familiar with the Cotswold escarpment will soon realize that constructing a canal down it was not an easy prospect. A route was found but it required 43 locks in 45 km (28 miles) and a monstrous tunnel running between Sapperton in the Frome Valley above Stroud, Gloucestershire, and Coates near to the official source of the River Thames. The

Kempsford, Gloucestershire

The serpentine course of the Thames writhes gently between the green and brown trees of the early spring arable landscape under the gaze of Kempsford church, built by John of Gaunt in 1390. Around the church, the evergreen and ancient yews remain as tantalizing evidence of pre-Christian purpose in this sacred site; the Iron Age Hwiccians and Saxons engaged in battle here. The village of Kempsford lies to the right of the church, as do the former Thames and Severn canal and RAF Fairford.

Sapperton Tunnel was about 3490 m (3816 yd) long and a formidable prospect for builders and bargees alike. The heyday of the Thames and Severn Canal lasted only until the nineteenth-century penetration of the railways.

At Inglesham, where the River Coln also enters the Thames, the clear trout-rich waters of the high Cotswold Hills above Bibury and Brockhampton flow sweetly into the dark river. Here is a taste of the northern Cotswolds and the classic landscape of Arlington Row with its luscious intimacy of stone building and marshy watercourses. Here, too, the crafty trout have inherited the knack of knowing the hook from the mayfly.

On to Lechlade and Buscot

Doubled and more purposeful now, the River Thames flows towards its last major Cotswold habitation, the town of Lechlade. The name comes from a combination of the River Leach and 'lade', meaning to load. Many loads have come and gone here in the past, not least the massive amounts of salt carried by pack horse trains from Droitwich in Cheshire down the Old Salt Way. This gateway to the Cotswolds is a very interesting town, although unfortunately far from quiet these days thanks to the lorries that negotiate its narrow streets. Lechlade's stone buildings and spired church mark the limit of navigation for most boats. In historic terms it was a wharf for the shipment of country produce, particularly cheese and stone, to Oxford and London.

Lechlade has a splendid stone toll bridge that is now controlled by traffic lights. Thames Path walkers crossing the bridge into town continue to benefit from the revolt in 1839 which forced the owners to remove the halfpenny toll for pedestrians. Lechlade is a relatively large town for the upper Thames, and has been a settlement since 2500 BC. There was Bronze Age development around 1700 BC, Celtic and Romano-British farmers both left traces and Saxon artefacts have also been found. The town has a strong association with the poet Percy Bysshe Shelley, who composed works in the churchyard and once rowed up the river from Old Windsor with his mistress, Mary Godwin, and his friend, Thomas Love Peacock, in 1815.

Between Lechlade's dominating spire and St John's Bridge, Buscot, lies a splendid straight church path, flanked by hedges and crossing the meadows. It must once have led to the now lost St John's Priory behind the bridge and the wonderful old haunted Trout Inn. From the bridge to Buscot is another superb meadow, flanked to the east by tall poplars and complemented by the languid Thames, strong from the input of the Cole and Leach rivers.

The confluence of the Rivers Thames and Coln, Gloucestershire

This is a late spring view, at the confluence of the Thames with the River Coln, of a rapidly greening landscape scattered with may blossom and enlivened by the first cut of grass for silage. The Thames Path is clearly visible running past the graceful footbridge towards Lechlade. The entry of the former Thames and Severn Canal is marked by the curious, lighthouse-like building, known as the Inglesham Roundhouse, amidst the trees.

Lechlade, Gloucestershire

The magnificent spire of Lechlade church, a landmark of note for some distance in this flat landscape, informs the knowing that the upstream limit of navigation for most rivercraft is about to be reached. The town of Lechlade has given itself the title 'Gateway to the Cotswolds' and its position on the river, road and path lends credence to this claim. It was also an inland port for many years; a 'lading' or loading point for country produce, salt from Cheshire, Double Gloucester cheeses and stone from local quarries. The riverbanks here are generously open and friendly; visitors are given good welcomes and provision is made for gentle enjoyment of the water's edge. The Thames Path follows the southern bank, although most walkers would be foolish not to accept the refreshment offered by this ancient settlement.

Long before concrete became a common building material, Rafaelle Monti (who was best known for his marble sculptures), experimented with Portland cement because it matched the texture and colour of many Portland stone buildings, particularly in London. His concrete sculpture of Old Father Thames thus became a commercial exhibit at the 1851 Great Exhibition, survived the fire that melted the Crystal Palace in 1936 and was bought by the Thames Conservancy for erection at Thames Head in 1958. Its wanderings continued because of alleged abuses from the students of the Royal Agricultural College and it was finally glued on to the lockside at St John's in 1974 for safe keeping.

Downstream from St John's Bridge begins the 3035-hectare (7500-acre) landholding of the National Trust's Buscot Estate, which includes not only Buscot house and grounds but also the model village and farmland. The church dates from 1200 and its Perpendicular tower makes the Queen Anne parsonage beside it look like a doll's house.

Buscot Park has gardens laid out by the landscaper Harold Peto but its finest hour probably came in 1879, under the management of an Australian called Robert Campbell. He soon turned the estate over to alcohol production from irrigated sugar-beet and beetroot crops. A distillery was built by the Thames and a narrow gauge railway was set up to move the beets to the riverside. Some of the alcohol made its way downstream to France for brandy production but, like most dreams, it eventually had to end. Buscot Estate includes its own hillfort at Badbury Hill, and the awesome Great Tithe Barn at Great Coxwell. There is a picnic area, with parking, near Buscot Weir pool.

The world cheese-shipping record for 1809 probably resided at Buscot when 3000 tonnes (3000 tons) of cheese were sent off from a minute wharf (now a National Trust car park). Opposite this squats a grey reminder of one of concrete's other uses – a Second World War pillbox which was part of a defensive frontier along the Thames and built in case the Nazis invaded Southern England.

Heaven on earth

Between Buscot and Kelmscot, Thames Path walkers will occasionally be lost behind high green walls of maize in places where the river alluvium provides a succulent anchorage. On reaching the village of Kelmscot the eighteenth century lives on in a remarkable preservation of the traditional Cotswold oolitic stone dwellings and cottage gardens bounded by dry stone walls. The village is a genuine act of survival, placed slightly away from the flood-prone Thames and its path, but close enough to belong to its ambience.

St John's Bridge, Oxfordshire

The counties of Gloucestershire, Wiltshire and Oxfordshire meet near St John's Lock, which is also the home of Rafaelle Monti's statue of Old Father Thames. The river is popular here for mooring up, especially close to the riverside lawns of the old Trout Inn to the Gloucestershire side of the bridge. The Thames Path will cut through the scene diagonally from bottom left to top right of the photograph, crossing under the road and over the river at the old ferry point called Bloomers Hole. A footbridge is being proposed here, to arch over the river adjacent to the row of tall poplars. The Thames is strengthened here by its junction with the Rivers Leach and Cole. The National Trust's Buscot Estate begins on the right.

A peaceful Thames

In the upper reaches of the Thames there are many quiet and lonely stretches where Thames Path walkers or fishermen may not see another human being for many hours. In the winter season especially, boats are a rarity but by early spring holiday hirers are ready for business and the river can become extremely busy. The River Thames Society, one of the many voluntary bodies dedicated to boating and caring for the river, was one of the instigators of the move to create the Thames Path.

A short step from the bank is Kelmscott Manor, where scholar, artist and *bon vivant* William Morris lived from 1871. Morris thought it heaven on earth and in its rural fold indulged his escapist aestheticism and shut out the growing industrial world. The harmonious life did not last long. Dante Gabriel Rossetti was joint tenant with Morris and often came to paint Jane Morris, but a friction developed that did not heal and Rossetti left for good in 1874 after a drug-induced row with some local fishermen. Kelmscott Manor is now a shrine to Morris and the Arts and Crafts Movement, but is only open on a few days of the year. The Arts and Crafts Movement was responsible for a modern revival of folk music, old English traditions, vernacular architecture and the artistry of cottage gardening.

Morris' grave can be visited in the Norman churchyard of St George's, Kelmscot, where his body was borne in a yellow haywain decorated with willow and vines. His vision of a Utopian life of harmony with natural beauty can still be felt and appreciated at Kelmscot.

The oldest bridge on the Thames

While Kelmscot is green and decked with the white-flecked bushes of hawthorn and may blossom in spring, and the river winds confidently through wilder banks, home to yellow flag irises and reed warblers, Radcot Bridge is a stone-based location rooted in its masculine battle-torn and quarrying history. It is one of those odd places on the Thames where the past seems to intrude on the present. Here sits the oldest existing bridge on the Thames, in the style of the thirteenth century, built in creamy local Taynton stone. This was the wharf from which such stone was sent to the stone masons of St Paul's Cathedral, and thousands of tons of it were brought laboriously by cart from Taynton quarry to Radcot before journeying by barge to London. Radcot was said to have had a bridge in 958, and there are two here now. The younger one was built by the Thames Commissioners and given a new lock so the old bridge could be bypassed.

Old Radcot Bridge has two pointed arches and a rounded middle one. The arch in the middle was originally pointed too but it was dismantled in 1388 by Henry Bolingbroke (who became Henry IV 11 years later) as a trap to catch royal favourite Robert de Vere, who was galloping south from Oxford on his way to support Richard II against Henry. The plan worked after a fashion – various knights were stabbed in the river and Robert de Vere had to shed his horse, armour and sword to swim for it. He escaped under cover of darkness.

North of the bridge is a rectangular earthwork called The Garrison which was

Kelmscot, Oxfordshire

The Cotswold stone of the village of Kelmscot, set in a sea of green abundance, makes this Thames-side village special but its association with William Morris turns it into part of British culture. Kelmscott Manor (note Morris' special spelling), which was Morris' home for many years in the late nineteenth century, is the impressive cluster of buildings on the far right of the picture. After his death in Hammersmith in 1896 William Morris was buried in the churchyard.

connected with the Civil War in 1645. The Garrison, however, is nothing compared to the nearby Faringdon Folly erected by Lord Berners, the musician and writer, in 1936. He requested that when he died he should be stuffed and seated at a grand piano at the very top of the tall folly, where he would be seen for miles around through the lighthouse-style windows. Sadly, his wish was never granted.

The Cotswold landscape

The Thames splits at Radcot Bridge, with the southern unnavigable fork leading to the ford at nearby Duxford. There are few settlements here, contrasting strongly with the many towns built downstream which developed into great trading centres and thriving communities. A flood-prone and deceitful Thames may explain why habitation was favoured less at Radcot Bridge (with the exception of the excellent pub) than other ancient crossing points and why Faringdon, with its drier, safer viewpoint, proved to be a greater attraction. The tree-girt knoll around the Faringdon Folly dominates the southern skyline from the Thames Path and gives just a hint of the rolling bulk of the Berkshire Downs. It was a defensible place where the prospects were good and refuge attainable.

Bampton, a town to the north of the river and renowned for its alleged invention of Morris dancing, had its own subtle defences – no one could find it. It was formerly called Bampton-in-the-Bush and for many years was only accessible by footpaths through impenetrable scrub. Some of the footpaths are still there but the bushes and the quasi-Australian addition to Bampton's name have long given way to wider fields and arable vistas. Thames Path walkers may be surprised and delighted to see Morris dancers at various inns along the river, where the jingling of bells and the swilling of ale provides a continuity with a rediscovered English past.

The Cotswolds give birth to the Thames but they never overwhelm it with their abrupt dissected plateaux or escarpment landscapes which are conjured up in the mind's eye whenever the Cotswolds are mentioned. The river does not know these places and in happy juvenile ignorance sets off to make its own name. The Cotswolds Area of Outstanding Natural Beauty (AONB) is a fitting place for the Thames Path to start (or finish), because of its sheer contrast with the great urban landscape of London, which bruises the senses with escarpments of brick dissected by roaring streams of traffic. The gentle dipping Cotswolds are in harmony; a balancing act between agriculture and habitation that forever seems just right for the human soul, a landscape that glows in the sunlight and warms the spirit.

Duxford, Oxfordshire

The Thames Path splits south of the hamlet of Chimney; the navigable route follows the Shifford Lock cut but the true river meanders towards Duxford. The tree-shaded fording place is clearly seen as a lip beneath the smooth brown surface of the river. While Shifford Lock is being built, the Thames Path will follow the footpath alongside the river to Duxford before deviating southwards to rejoin the river at Tenfoot Bridge.

Oxfordshire Thames

The river and the path's edge grow wilder and deeper here, with habitation dictated by the Thames' tendency to flood. The roads also retreat to dry ground and causeways, often following Celtic and Roman trackways. Ferry, ford and footbridge all have their finest hour here. South beyond the gluey clays or shifting pea shingle of the Vale of the White Horse, through which the Thames Path now strolls, can be seen the northern face of the Berkshire Downs, and beyond the rounded wooded breasts of Boars Hill and Wytham Woods can be glimpsed the dim shadow of the Chiltern Hills. More solid than a shadow stands Didcot Power Station, and further downriver Swinford tollbridge stops the traffic for its twopenny tax. Even before the Thames rounds the corner into the intellectual embrace of Oxford its valley has become quite worldly. From its looking-glass mere dribblings through Lewis Carroll's wonderland and inspirational Oxford, the river becomes less certain of its course and twists south, east and west through Abingdon, Dorchester and Wallingford. These historic towns, keepers of crucial moments in England's secret past, are unafraid of their wet charge but wisely step to one side of it just in case it becomes unruly. Above them all sit Wittenham Clumps, sentinels of the Chiltern Hills and guardians of the Goring Gap.

For users of the Thames Path, the entrance to Oxfordshire clings low to a wide valley where pollarded willows and poplars mark time with passing feet. There is a peace here despite the visual distractions provided by Didcot Power Station and the aerial gyrations of RAF aeroplanes as they fly into Brize Norton or Abingdon airfield. Fishermen and pleasure cruisers may be the only human companions for many miles in these parts.

Walkers in need of rest or refreshment could take a few short sideways detours to places that have their own rewards, and one of the most interesting is Stanton Harcourt. Three towers dominate this village: that of the squat Perpendicular

Stanton Harcourt, Oxfordshire

Lying slightly away from the river, Stanton Harcourt is a settlement dominated by the three grey stone towers of its church and manor house. The church stands four-square and proud abutting the large stew pond, which formerly provided the village with carp in times of need. The two separated towers of the manor house were once joined as part of a much larger residence. Alexander Pope set a translation of Homer's *The Iliad* to verse in the central tower and it now bears his name.

church, the isolated Pope's Tower and the one belonging to the largest intact medieval kitchen in Britain. The church is set amidst a landscape of stew (fish) ponds, part of both local commoners' rights of piscary and a major element of the food supply of the Harcourt family seat in times past. Pope's Tower was once connected to the vast kitchen tower by the, now demolished, manor house. The seventeenth-century English poet, Alexander Pope, passed some time here while he turned a translation of Homer's *Iliad* into elegant verse.

From Pope's window a line of sight as straight as a ley line can be seen eastwards across the Thames, through the cleft right into the heart of Oxford's Carfax. Between the hills, especially when the sunlight plays upon the distant stonework, lies a clutch of colleges, spires and church towers, providing a view little changed perhaps since the seventeenth century. It has been said that there is a Harcourt tradition of taking out the tops of trees on the old estate boundary so these magnificent views of Oxford can be preserved. The Harcourt family still lives here in a remarkable lineage that stretches back centuries.

Thames crossing points

Walkers returning to the riverside and the Thames Path will reach the ancient crossing point called Bablock Hythe. This place has never been bridged, although until recently a ferry and its attendant hubbub had been here for a thousand years. About 0.8 km (½ mile) from the river, hidden in the bushy hedgerows of the old straight track that leads eastwards from the ferry to the centre of Oxford, is the Physic Well. On a bleak midwinter's day under grey skies, the brooding thorns seem to cluster protectively around this spot. The Physic Well, now just a muddy spring, unkempt and uncared for, is an important local place of great antiquity and was once a source of healing waters. William Morris and Matthew Arnold both knew Bablock Hythe: Arnold's poem 'The Scholar Gypsy' and Morris' book *News from Nowhere* contain lyric descriptions of the ferry point and its countryside.

It is still a puzzle why some Thames crossing points and not others developed into major places of habitation. Accidents of history and strategic changes in patterns of trade routes are often cited but the sheer unpredictability of the winter floods must have had a great impact on the Oxfordshire Thames. The riversides were abandoned to the lonely ferrymen, eel catchers and occasional inn keepers despite the economic potential to be derived from the passing trade.

The Trout Inn, Godstow, Oxfordshire

Here is an example of the happy consequences of the conjunction of rivers and roads as channels of communication. The Trout at Godstow is a twelfth-century representative of all the excellent inns and hostelries to be found at such points along the Thames – conveniently threaded together for users of the Thames Path. The Trout was originally built as a hospice for Godstow Nunnery, which occupied the opposite bank of the Thames.

TROUT INN

Towards Godstow

From Bablock Hythe the Thames Path begins a great sweep, following the river around Wytham Woods past Farmoor Reservoir, Pinkhill lock and under the Swinford bridge until, heading south through the meadows of Pixey and Yarnton, it reaches Godstow.

'God's place', from which Godstow receives its name, could be an apt description for many a favourite stretch of the riverside country of the Thames. Only a few ruins now remain of the once famous Godstow Nunnery founded here.

Rosamund Clifford, 'Fair Rosamund', who was Henry II's mistress, spent her final years at Godstow until her death in 1176. Many myths and legends have been woven around Rosamund's life: her name was certainly Clifford but it was Henry II who called her 'Rose of the World' (*Rosa Mundi*). Despite popular belief she was not poisoned by his jealous wife Eleanor, nor did she live in a secret bower hidden in a maze. However, in nearby Woodstock in what are now the grounds of Blenheim Palace, there was once an older palace that did contain a Rosamund's Bower and a Fair Rosamund's Well.

Godstow Nunnery looks cold and forlorn today, having been dismantled by Parliamentary forces during the Civil War, but its ground plan is retained by its outer limestone walls which still stand next to the Thames Path in a verdant riverside setting. Here at Port Meadow, opposite Godstow, is the simple, green and natural counterpoint to the vertical and intellectually inspired richness of the city of Oxford which sets this place apart from all others in the landscape of the Thames Valley. It should be regarded as a national treasure.

The approach to Oxford

When a visiting American professor in Oxford asked to be shown the most ancient institution in the city he was taken to the common land of Port Meadow. Although it bears traces from the Bronze Age, the name 'Port' is a clear indicator of its Saxon use, meaning 'a trading place'. It is now a Site of Special Scientific Interest and carries extensive common rights to graze cattle, horses and geese. Its ownership is obscure, although the people of Oxford enjoy legal rights of access over its entire 178 hectares (440 acres). In the winter, when freeze follows flood, this vast planar

Looking to Port Meadow from Godstow, Oxfordshire

The flat green expanse of Port Meadow on the left of the photograph is notable for its vast size, which contrasts acutely with the well-farmed land on the right-hand side of the Thames. Port Meadow is ancient common land protected forever by public rights of access and extensive common rights to graze cattle, horses and geese. The Thames Path follows the right-hand side of the river along the established towpath past the old walls of Godstow Nunnery.

Christ Church, Oxford

Christ Church Cathedral was built on the site of St Frideswide's Priory, which is possibly the oldest part of the city of Oxford. The cathedral dates from the twelfth century but has been subsumed by Christ Church College and its massive, formally landscaped, Tom Quad. Christ Church also owns meadows running down to the Thames, where college barges used to be a great feature in the nineteenth century. Some of Oxford's other colleges can be seen in the background, with apparently little modern building to interrupt the golden stone of this city of dreaming spires.

landscape becomes a skating rink and a giant mirror for Oxford's dreaming spires, as Thomas Hardy called them in his novel *Jude the Obscure*.

On the opposite bank is Binsey, with its old hostelry and the well and church of St Margaret. The curative well waters and saint were reputed to cure diseases of the eye. It was on a boat trip upstream past Binsey to Godstow on 4 July 1862 that Charles Dodgson (Lewis Carroll) first told the story of *Alice in Wonderland* to the Liddell family. It is also believed that the countryside that inspired the chess board in *Alice through the Looking Glass* was Otmoor, east of Oxford, with its chequered pattern of arable wheat and grassland divided by drains and ditches.

The Thames and Isis

Gradually the Thames Path reaches Oxford, although the city has visually announced itself from some considerable distance. The name 'Ox-ford' is obviously derived from a crossing point for cattle, but its exact location is keenly disputed. There is even a dispute about the name of the river, which in Oxford is clearly named 'Isis'. This is not unique to Oxford but has become institutionalized here. Why this should be is a mystery but the whole river from the source bears the alternative name of Isis. Some people have suggested that Old Father Thames and Mother Isis are just images associated with the river, but it has also been called a 'strong brown god', an 'infant' and a 'stripling', according to its physical character at various points along its course. These anthropomorphic images are vividly portrayed in literature and sculpture even to this day.

Julius Caesar called the river Tamesis, but various spellings have appeared since then, 'Tamyse' being popular in Anglo-Saxon times. Only since about 1600 has 'Thames' become the standard spelling. We have to go back, past the pan-European Celtic era, even to obtain a meaning for the word Thames. Most etymologists now agree it is derived from the Sanskrit (ancient Indian) word 'tamasa', meaning dark river or dark water. Use of the word may have been spread from India through the Celts to Britain. The Thames drainage basin is scattered with Celtic settlement names (ending in -dun, -don or -ton, such as London).

In and around Oxford

The image of Oxford is one of a city and university that hides behind historical enigmas and stone façades; a massive intellectual factory tucked behind college gates, high walls and secret gardens.

Oxford is believed to have originated as a settlement around St Frideswide's Priory in the eighth century. It still has a Saxon building (St Michael's Tower, 1050) from its old function as the crossroads of England and has inherited its Saxon street plan with Carfax at its centre. In 1066 it was the sixth largest town in England and so five years later the Normans built the castle to control it and the river traffic. It was from the castle that Queen Matilda made her famous white-cloaked dash across a snowy, frozen Thames to Wallingford and freedom. The university was grafted on to

Oxford in the thirteenth century, when it thus became a city. Merton College was the first, being founded in 1264. After the thirteenth century, however, Oxford declined as the Head of the River; the Black Death and dwindling trade allowed the commercial centre to be acquired by the expanding colleges. Tension resulted and some of the riots between town and gown were deadly and serious. The scholars often complained to the king and, unfairly, the colleges' privileges were extended.

The eighteenth century saw the emergence of Oxford's most glorious architectural period, particularly through the works of Nicholas Hawksmoor, the celebrated architect and freemason. The Oxford Canal, built to connect London via the Thames to the newly industrial Midlands was constructed by James Brindley in 1790. Other transport followed: the railways arrived and then (the mechanical) William Morris opened a bicycle shop in 1902 at 48 High Street. By 1913 he had produced his first car, the Morris Oxford. Since then the endearing Morris Minor has become part of Britain's cultural heritage.

Oxford has some fascinating buildings and marvellous contents, such as the Clarendon Building, Bodleian Library and the Ashmolean Museum. One of the best known buildings is Christ Church, which was built over the original St Frideswide's Priory, named after the eighth-century princess whose lusty suitor was magically blinded and then restored to sight by a visit to St Margaret's Well at Binsey. Christ Church College's most famous occupant, Charles Dodgson, taught maths here and, writing under the name of Lewis Carroll, invented *Alice in Wonderland et al* for his own princess, the young Alice Liddell.

Although the Thames Path can be followed relatively easily through Oxford's riverside buildings there seems to be little point in rushing past such a precious amalgam of stone and time. Any exploration of Oxford will be a delight.

South of the junction with the River Cherwell and Magdalen's fritillary meadows, Thames Path walkers will be surprised by the extent of the green meadows squeezed into Oxford's urban frame. An enormous green wedge of reed beds and grazed alluvial meadows drives into the city, much of it protected as wildlife habitat by the City Council and the Berkshire, Buckinghamshire and Oxfordshire Naturalists' Trust. College barges and delicate wooden bridges are still to be seen on some stretches and the Oxford rowing events, Summer Eights or Torpids, cause great excitement among the undergraduate rowing fraternity. When walking this path no one should forget the novel *Zuleika Dobson*, which Max Beerbohm wrote in 1911, and the tragedy caused by the eponymous heroine during Eights Week!

Much of the land around Oxford is already held in protective trust but it would be interesting to think that a green ring of woodland might one day be planted around it as a small-scale 'community forest' to physically reinforce Oxford's green belt.

At Iffley, history reasserts itself and all Thames Path walkers should make the detour to St Mary's Church to view the splendid carvings incised into the Norman stonework. Here be dragons, demons and all manner of mythical beasts.

The movable village

Between Iffley and Nuneham the river is channelled southwards in a recognizable valley. Agriculture here is more of a big field operation, with fewer grass leys or hedgerow trees, and a crop of electricity pylons marching away towards Didcot. Relatively high above the Thames and commanding the river bluffs sits Nuneham Park, built in 1756. An entire village had to be removed and resettled in model quarters alongside a nearby road to satisfy the landscaping contract. This act earned the opprobrium of the eighteenth-century poet and writer Oliver Goldsmith, who penned perhaps his most famous poem, 'The Deserted Village', because of it. To accompany the Palladian house, the grounds were laid out by another equally famous figure of the eighteenth century, Capability Brown, for the first Earl of Harcourt. The private chapel was built in the style of a classical temple and its green copper-domed roof is a landmark. Today, the model cottages are plagued more by the incessant traffic on the A423 than by social iniquity.

In the grounds of Nuneham, which is visible from the Thames, is the Carfax Conduit, a very ornately carved stone cistern of 1616 that once stood at Carfax in the middle of Oxford. When in use it was an elaborate water dispenser, drawing fresh water from a reservoir outside the city. There was class distinction apparent in its use; first dip went to the university scholars and the overflow went to the common people – another source of rivalry between town and gown.

The historic town of Abingdon

Below Nuneham, which was another boating destination of Charles Dodgson and Alice Liddell, the river and path curl beneath Lock Wood and the Oxford-Paddington railway bridge and run head on into Abingdon. The path's route crosses from the north to the south bank and the river is artificially looped around Andersey Island. All of Abingdon's development lies to the north of the river and the southern bank is green, open and greatly used for recreation.

Abingdon is one of the most important of all the historic towns on the Thames and it hosts some strange events. First comes the Morris-dancing battle dating from 1700, held between the men of Ock Street and the men of the Vineyard for the horns of a black ox. These days, on the nearest Saturday to 19 June, the whole town is given up to a weekend of Morris dancing, during which the dancers elect a Mayor of Ock Street. Second, residents still follow the tradition, dating from the coronation of George III in 1760, that decrees buns should be thrown from the County Hall on all similar occasions. As coronations are not all that frequent the urge for bun-throwing

Folly Bridge, Oxford

FACING PAGE Folly Bridge lies just upstream from Christ Church Meadow and is always popular with people on the river. As a break from walking, Thames Path users might try hiring a punt from the boatyard next to the bridge. Sir Francis Bacon lived in the old drawbridge gatehouse which gives the bridge its name, although the structure was demolished in 1779.

Nuneham House, Nuneham Courtenay, Oxfordshire

OVERLEAF Surrounded by a patchwork quilt of yellow rape fields and green parkland, Nuneham House sits firmly in its landscaped gardens high above the Thames and the developing valley. The Carfax Conduit, which is a stone public fountain, was moved from Carfax in the centre of Oxford to the grounds here in 1786 and is just visible through the trees from the Thames Path.

breaks out at the slightest reasonable excuse – and it keeps the mallards happy on the river too.

Abingdon's brewing history began with the Abbey monks, of which the modern-day Morland's Brewery is a descendant. The Abbey itself, once a seat of enormous wealth and power, was crushed in the Dissolution and very little now remains. The whole town has grown around this institution, which was founded in 675.

Clifton Hampden and the Sinodun Hills

South of Abingdon and into the flat lands of gravel outwash, the river cuts deep into Culham Reach before pirouetting a full 90 degrees to the east. The Thames Path follows the cut and avoids the complicated Sutton Pools. Under the Oxford-Paddington railway again, and studiously ignoring Didcot, the river wriggles into Long Wittenham, although the path leads straight to Clifton Hampden along the Clifton Cut.

Clifton Hampden's church of St Michael and All Angels, which was renovated by Henry Gibbs after 1842 (when he bought the whole village), stands on a little mound over the river's edge. It is an old site and a former ferry point, although a brick bridge was built in 1867, allegedly from a design sketched on a shirt cuff by the architect, Sir George Gilbert Scott, who restored or designed many of Britain's landmarks, including the Albert Memorial.

By contrast to the quiet village, the new power of the nuclear age is being tested not far away in Culham, at a vast white temple of a building that houses the Joint European Torus (JET), an experiment in hot plasma nuclear fusion.

A little way along the river at Long Wittenham, the Thames follows a wide curve, leaving a flat apron of land showing evidence of former occupation by Iron Age and Bronze Age settlers. Rising above it, and approached by a long line of statuesque poplars, are possibly the oldest recorded tree clumps in Britain. They sit on the dual hillocks of the Sinodun Hills that still bear their Celtic name and are graced not only by the trees but also by an Iron Age hillfort. This place was very important in Celtic times and only from the summit of the Wittenham Clumps (or Berkshire Bubs as they are sometimes called) can it be appreciated how much strategic territory they surveyed: high above the Rivers Thames and Thame, not far from the Ridgeway and Icknield Way, within sight of White Horse Hill and at the border between the Catuvellauni and the Atrebati factions of Iron Age Britain.

The Temple at Nuneham House, Nuneham Courtenay, Oxfordshire

The grounds of Nuneham House contain the copper-domed church of All Saints, designed by 'Athenian' Stuart as a classical temple and now surrounded by an arboretum of splendid specimen trees, including a sticky fruiting mulberry of great age. The temple was used in one of the episodes of the popular television series, *Inspector Morse.*

Childe Beale Wildlife Park, Berkshire

Thames Path walkers passing through the leafy hillside opposite Childe Beale will see any number of exotic animals and birds grazing in the fields below. Childe Beale has a spectacular collection of rare pheasants as well as a much loved children's corner. The main concentration of facilities is within the woods and lakes sandwiched in the wedge between the Thames and the London-Bristol railway line. Visible on the island in the centre of the photograph is a building containing a display of modern and antique model boats which reflect the association with passing river craft. The Goring Gap has been the main communication route for all forms of transport, both north and south of the Berkshire Downs, for millennia.

The Clumps are owned by the Northmoor Trust and managed as a nature reserve and public access land. In the little car park is a lump of local stone discreetly carved with a rose, where every year the Chairman of Oxfordshire County Council presents the Trust with a single red rose as its token payment for the public use of the land.

There are ancient pubs in Long Wittenham and Clifton Hampden that exude cosiness and antiquity, with their gardens flopping on to the banks of the Thames. The Plough earns a special mention in *Three Men in a Boat*. The Thames Path follows the curving river and runs through and over Day's Lock, courtesy of the National Rivers Authority and a newly created section of footpath. The temptation to explore Dorchester or Wittenham Clumps should be acceded to at this point.

Historic Dorchester

If you peel away just a few layers of history, the Celts and Romans live on in Dorchester. The town is archaeologically dominated by the Celtic hillfort over the river on the Sinodun Hills and the defensive double earthworks called the Dyke Hills. The Romans founded their military settlement close to the junction of the rivers Thames and Thame and called it Dorcina Castra. This fort was built over a much earlier strategic location and better protected the Roman road, then new, from Silchester. Romano-British and Anglo-Saxon settlers built a town from the ruins after the fifth-century Roman withdrawal.

St Birinius came to Dorchester in the company of the King of Northumbria in 635 to baptize the heathen King Cynegils of Wessex in the River Thame. This act converted much of southern Britain to Christianity at a stroke. The first abbey here was succeeded by the abbey-church of St Peter and St Paul, which is still used as a spectacularly large parish church. Delicious home-made teas are available most weekends at the abbey gatehouse – an excellent end to any local walk. The path to Day's Lock past the Dyke Hills is popular and the lock keeper usually has a box of Pooh sticks for sale (on behalf of the Royal National Lifeboat Institution) for dropping into the river from the bridge.

From Wittenham Clumps the historical picture can still be clearly imagined, although some spectacular archaeological features, such as the Dorchester cursus, have now been destroyed by the water-filled gravel pits which surround the village. The Thame enters the main stream near here and the Thames ceases to be given its alternative title of Isis.

Wittenham Clumps, Oxfordshire

Commanding the entrance to the Goring Gap and visible over long distances in the Vale of the White Horse, the Wittenham Clumps are said to be the oldest tree clumps in Britain. They have suffered extensive tree loss for a number of reasons and are being replanted in a systematic manner by the Northmoor Trust. The Sinodun Hills on which they stand are a natural defensive site and were once the home of an Iron Age hillfort.

The landscape and settlement pattern between Dorchester and Wallingford was once dictated by marshy ground and the attempts to drain it. Habitation still clings to ribbons of higher ground or Roman roadsides, or fringes spectacularly large village greens such as at Warborough. Willows are still regularly cropped by pollarding and attendant cordwood piles at careful intervals mark the run of ditches and drains. Huddled umbrella-canopied fishermen mimic the stacking pattern of the wooden piles in their quest for fish.

Crossing the Thames to Benson and Ewelme

The Thames Path switches banks once again at the village of Benson. There is an active marina with plenty of boats available for hire, but the place is better known for its RAF base. The village reached its zenith as a coaching stop in the early nineteenth century but it has a long history and was formerly called Bensington.

Beyond Benson and just over the hill is Ewelme, the last resting place of Jerome Klapka Jerome who immortalized boat trips on the Thames in his comic novel *Three Men in a Boat*. Ewelme is a splendid place in which to be buried and a dignified village in which to live. It nestles around its own Cow Common, bubbling spring and verdant watercress beds, and the villagers fought tooth and nail to be recognized as part of the Chilterns Area of Outstanding Natural Beauty – and won. However, it didn't stop the local gravel extraction nor the waste disposal consents from creeping ever closer.

After Benson, the river and its path dive powerfully southwards through deep but fast eroding alluvium – a factor that will cause problems unless bank protection is provided at some expense in the future. The Thames Path slips past the site of Wallingford Castle, now just a few humps in a farmstead, and enters the attractive riverside town of Wallingford between tethered cruisers and parkland railings. The riverside church and distinctive open spire of St Peter's is a prominent landmark dating from 1777. Many of the town's listed buildings also date from this period.

Looking towards the Chiltern landscape

Wallingford has had a turbulent history and is a lively place, although it is a dreadful traffic bottleneck today, having inherited a Saxon town plan fit for pack horses but less suitable for lorries. Like Abingdon, it is a lop-sided town with all its development on one bank of the river, seemingly braced for attack from the direction of London and using the Thames as a moat. The market place and its stately seventeenth-century Town Hall are worth a detour. The national headquarters of the British Trust for Conservation Volunteers lies a short distance from the square.

The Thames Path wends southwards, through churchyard and alleyway, towards the rising bulk of the Chiltern escarpment. Settlements are sparse to the east, where massive undulating arable fields of wheat and barley ripple in summer winds towards the beech wood skyline. The ancient courses of the Upper and Lower

Icknield Ways run parallel to the river for a while and are crossed at right angles by the deep boundary earthwork called Grims Ditch, which is now occupied by the Ridgeway National Trail.

Moulsford and South Stoke are the last paired (but unconnected) settlements that both lie in Oxfordshire on opposite sides of the river. A new right of way will be created here to take the Thames Path under Isambard Kingdom Brunel's nineteenth-century viaduct of the Paddington-Bristol railway.

The Oxfordshire Thames shows an increasingly sophisticated well-watered landscape of farmland and alluvial richness punctuated by orange balsam, ladies smock, water mint and meadowsweet in the riverside meadows and ditches. It is culturally enhanced by its elegant towns of Oxford, Abingdon and Wallingford, which, in turn, depended for their growth and existence on the track system and crossing points of the river which so influenced the British nation at small but crucial moments. Great crested grebes dive for food in waters that for millennia have been pivotal in our political and cultural development.

Chiltern Thames

In the chalky Goring Gap the Thames follows its gentle groove between the Berkshire Downs and the Chilterns with grace and restrained, chalk-corseted sinuosity. It bulges out a little near Reading, but is pushed back into shape by the rivers Kennet and Loddon. These reaches are the classic Thames haunts of Jerome K Jerome's *Three Men in a Boat* and Kenneth Grahame's *The Wind in the Willows*; of swan-upping and Pimms-downing; of Stanley Spencer and Henry Taunt. Here, perhaps, is the quintessential Thames. The landscape is pleasingly wooded and pleasantly farmed, although becoming more pheasanty as pure agriculture changes from being a necessity to more of a hobby. Reading, of beer, bulbs and biscuits fame, is the largest town on this stretch but opposed in its expansion by the rural tongue of Southern Oxfordshire which blows its raspberry from north of the river. Along the Thames and up the Loddon past Twyford dwells the rare summer snowflake, the beautiful Loddon lily. Herons and vast flocks of Canada geese fly overhead round here. None of these, however, is as exotic as the international visitors to Henley's less than secret regatta. The town goes mad for two weeks, culminating in spectacular fireworks, then reverts to its customary, sleepy repose once more – a mood that generally befits the Chiltern Thames.

Goring and Streatley is a paired Thames settlement, sitting at one of the narrowest parts of the Thames Valley, where the dangers of flooding have always been less severe than in the flatter wider areas. This is an historic Roman and pre-Roman crossing point (although probably not the only fording point of the Icknield Way) and a modern crossroads for two Countryside Commission National Trails – the Thames Path and the Ridgeway.

In times past drovers forced flocks of sheep and herds of cattle through the water, and at least one major tragedy occurred with human traffic when a ferry overturned in 1674, drowning 15 men, women and children. Today the river is busy tumbling

Streatley, Berkshire

Streatley is one of the most significant places in the Thames Valley because it marks the point where the ancient Ridgeway meets the Thames. These two vital communication links served as nationally important trade routes until relatively recent times. Now, Streatley and its twin village of Goring are equally important as the junction of two of the Countryside Commission's National Trails – the Ridgeway and the Thames Path.

Clifton Hampden, Oxfordshire

The dignified village of Clifton Hampden, with its thatched cottages and ancient pubs, is just a small detour away from the line of the Thames Path. Access is gained by crossing the red brick bridge built in 1864–7 in imitation Norman style from a sketch made on a shirt cuff by Sir George Gilbert Scott. The church of St Michael and All Angels and, indeed, the whole village, was restored by Henry Gibbs after he bought the estate in 1842. Lurking in the background is the Joint European Torus (JET), which is experimenting with hot plasma fusion in an attempt to create limitless power by nuclear fusion. It is well supplied with electricity by Didcot Power Station nearby.

over weirs, sluices, locks and round the abutments of a splendidly low-level roller-coaster sort of bridge. An old barge from Magdalen College in Oxford is moored peacefully outside the Swan Inn and people are drawn to this ancient and significant place simply to watch it all.

With such importance as a place forged from the drama of its physical position, the Goring Gap has always reaped the benefits that come with the need to protect its landscape. Central to this role is the National Trust, which owns Lardon Chase to the west and The Holies, recently acquired, next to it. These hilltops offer magnificent views through the Gap of a winding Thames heading to the unseen sea and, to the north, the spread of the Vale of Oxford.

The surrounding landscape

This is the seam between two of Britain's most important blocks of landscape outside the National Parks. The Chilterns AONB to the east of the Thames covers 833 sq km (322 sq miles) and was confirmed in 1965, while the North Wessex Downs AONB to the west, confirmed in 1972, stretches over 1730 sq km (668 sq miles). Both areas are subject to protective policies to conserve and enhance their natural beauty, taking into account the needs of agriculture, forestry, rural industry and the economic and social needs of local communities. Sensitive sustainable development, whether it is quasi-industrial or recreational, is seen as one of the key ways in which the competing demands of modern society can be accommodated within these precious landscapes. There are now 39 AONBs covering nearly 14 per cent of the total land surface of England and Wales.

It is largely a measure of the success of the AONB landscape protection policies that there is a dramatic absence in the Goring Gap of those crude monstrosities which came with the Electric Age – pylons. In the surrounding non-AONB lands inhabited by Didcot Power Station, Harwell Nuclear Laboratory and the Joint European Torus at Culham, 400-kv power lines are strung around like hop poles. However, in a deliberate and thankful act of non-intrusion the electricity flows underground beneath the chalk downs of the Goring Gap.

Between Goring and Mapledurham, the river, path, railway and main road all squeeze together between chalk hills that seem like mountains, given the flatness of the preceding Oxfordshire clay vale. The Chiltern beech woods mingle with wheat

Goring Gap, Berkshire and Oxfordshire

It is easy to see why this landscape deserves the accolade of Area of Outstanding Natural Beauty (AONB). The Thames is the feature common to both the Chilterns AONB, to the right of the photograph, and the North Wessex Downs AONB, to the left, all the way through the Goring Gap. Here at Basildon, the birthplace of seventeenth-century agricultural pioneer Jethro Tull, the erosive power of the Thames is concentrated upon the chalk of the Chiltern Hills, leaving a wide flat floodplain on the North Wessex Downs side. This landscape is being utilized for conservation and recreational purposes in the ownership of the Childe Beale Wildlife Trust. The sensitive management of the gravel-extracted lagoon as a refuge for wildfowl is exemplary. The Thames Path rises through the woods on the hillside to the right.

fields, and the valley floor is a deep green sward grazed by cattle, sheep and occasional wallabies – escapees from parks and now living wild in the Chilterns. The Thames Path makes its longest deviation away from the river here before entering Whitchurch. From Gatehampton the path (here a bridleway) has climbed high – at least 46 m (150 ft) above the river to give almost alpine views out from Hartslock Wood, then it sweeps down the hilly main street of Whitchurch to arrive at one of the two surviving toll bridges on the Thames. Thames Path walkers will be pleased to know that pedestrians don't have to pay to cross this bridge.

On to Pangbourne and Purley

Having crossed the Thames, walkers will soon reach the town of Pangbourne, which represented the end of the river for Jerome K Jerome in *Three Men in a Boat* when the lure of the Alhambra and a chop proved too much for the wet, dispirited trio (and dog). St James' Church has Berkshire's largest collection of hatchments, which bear the family coat of arms of the Breedons. Church Cottage was the home, in the last saddened years of his life, of Kenneth Grahame, author of *The Wind in the Willows* and one-time official at the Bank of England.

Crossing the white-painted iron toll bridge, the path continues along grassy but well-worn meadows, owned by the National Trust, towards the arc of the river containing Westbury Meads. On the northern bank lies Mapledurham House, sitting amidst a screen of mature parkland trees in the Country Park. Also hidden among the foliage is a working water mill recorded in Domesday and the church of St Margaret. The house still belongs to the same Blount family that built it in 1588.

Sadly, Mapledurham is inaccessible to Thames Path walkers, and so the path enters Purley on the southern bank. Purley is a problem for walkers because of riverside obstructions and it seems to have quite a history of such difficulties. In the nineteenth century Purley Magna estate was owned by a Major Storey who spent most of his time keeping people off the riverbank. His inevitable come-uppance arrived when he found a party of women picnicking on his land. Having thrown their entire meal, crockery and tablecloth into the river, the picnickers asked him to thank his wife for her kindness in loaning it all to them.

Mapledurham, Oxfordshire

Mapledurham House, together with the oldest working water mill on the Thames and the red-roofed church of St Margaret's, sits peacefully in mature parkland leading down from the Chiltern Hills to the water's edge. The Blount family built the house in 1588 and it has remained in their family ever since. Here is a melange of buildings and scenery indicative of the quality of the landscape in the Chilterns Area of Outstanding Natural Beauty.

The approach of Reading

This point marks the transition from the AONB-quality countryside to the suburban areas of west Reading. There is still a strong woodland presence here amongst the houses, up the valley of the River Pang and on the slopes behind Mapledurham. The Thames Path stays close to the water's edge underneath the railway embankment before breaking cover across the wide flood plain around Little John's Farm and the site of the annual Reading Rock Festival. The river and the Thames Path manage to squeeze through Reading's least urbanized areas and pass the riverside towerblock landmarks of Thames Water and the National Rivers Authority – the main partners in maintaining the river quality of the Thames catchment area.

In 870, however, water purity was of little consequence to Alfred the Great, who had just lost a battle to invading Danes in the fillet of water meadows between the rivers Kennet and Thames. Alfred got his own back in the following Battle of Aescendum on the Downs above Wantage.

Reading then surprisingly became known for religious relics: Henry I endowed his twelfth-century Reading Abbey with the mummified 'blessed hand of St James the Apostle', St Anne's Chapel, constructed on the old Thames bridge, held what was left of 'a piece of the halter Judas hanged himself with' and 'the blessed knife that killed St Edward'. What's more, the relics of St Anne's Chapel were believed to have been brought there by an angel with only one wing! Nearby, St Anne's Well was an important place of pilgrimage in the Middle Ages for people with diseases of the eye – echoes of the restorative well waters of Binsey and Oxford. Henry I was so fond of Reading that after his death his body was shipped back from Rouen in France for burial in the Abbey.

Leaving behind most of the urban areas and heading east between Reading and Sonning the river landscape is overcome by massive sheets of water – gravel workings in various stages of transition from what was originally meadowland. The scene is overlooked by the BBC monitoring station at Caversham House with its satellite dishes, and overawed by the British Gas gasometer at the junction with the Kennet and Avon Canal. The pretty woodlands of Sonning Scarp partially screen the Thames Valley Business Park which was built on the former site of the incongruous Earley Power Station. This section of the Thames Path is designated as one of the three main stretches of cyclepath.

Sonning, Berkshire

The Thames Path makes a striking sine-wave pattern as it approaches the village of Sonning from Reading. The maturity of this settlement and its old river crossing point means this is one of the classic stretches of middle-Thames scenery. The impact of trees in our appreciation of landscape is made clear by this clustering of habitation, trees and the water's edge. People enjoy the open access to the river here by the old water mill, which has been converted into a theatre.

Sonning and beyond

Sonning (which used to be pronounced 'Sunning') is the only place with a vehicular crossing between Reading and Henley and so its lovely eighteenth-century red-brick, hump-backed bridge suffers constantly from excess traffic. The Thames Path shares this bridge and the pavement is rather narrow but is approached from Sonning Lock by an excellent promenade. It is an old crossing point of the Thames and claimed early victory for the proto-conservationists William Holman Hunt and Sir Edwin Lutyens when it was under threat of demolition. Lutyens built a house here for Edward Hudson (then the owner of *Country Life* magazine) in 1901 on the site of the former dwelling of the Deans of Salisbury. It is, not surprisingly, called The Deanery and has a curious weather vane of a Dean preaching to empty pews. The Norman church, the quaint village, school, pub and mill (now a theatre-restaurant) mark it out as a special place.

Past Sonning and spoon-bending Uri Geller's riverside mansion the valley broadens where the swift-flowing Loddon meets the Thames. The path keeps to the rising ground on the chalky northern side, passing quietly beneath Shiplake College grounds. To the east is Wargrave, tucked into a tight bend of the river above an undeveloped homogeneously flat meadow crossed by the low viaduct which carries the railway branch line from Twyford to Henley-on-Thames.

Like Mapledurham, Wargrave is another manor mentioned in Domesday. It has a sombre-sounding name but a splendidly vibrant community. The heart of the village clusters around Mill Green and the church, which is hidden from both the river and the road. The green provides a setting for festivals, pancake races and other community festivities which are occasionally sponsored by the Sultan of Oman who owns the white-painted Wargrave Manor and its surrounding deer park. To add to the atmosphere, there is a traditional ghost in the Bull Inn. The Thames Path curves around the bend in the river on the opposite bank to the village but during the Wargrave Regatta an *ad hoc* ferry service operates from the George and Dragon pub to the towpath. Jerome K Jerome enjoyed a good landfall at the hostelry, famed in his day for its inn sign painted on two sides in two quite different styles by two quite different artists, George Leslie and Mr Hodgson, who were both members of the Royal Academy.

The village name derives from 'weirgrove' or 'weregrave', from its time as a settlement on the edge of Windsor Forest. Over the centuries it has had a secret store of emancipated women. Queen Emma, the 'Fair Maid of Normandy', was astute

Wargrave, Berkshire

Snow is a relatively rare winter visitor to the south of England, but the Chiltern Hills are fairly high and catch snowfalls that might have passed over elsewhere. The beauty of the winter landscape and the opaque sunlight towards the end of the day have combined here to cast the still water in bronze. The Twyford-Henley-on-Thames branch line crosses the river at Wargrave, adjacent to the boatyard. The Thames Path can be clearly seen as a thin black line close to the right-hand bank.

enough to marry both Saxon and Danish kings (Ethelred and Cnut respectively). She owned the manor a thousand years before the Suffragettes set fire to the church in 1914, which was not long after Marie (Madame) Tussaud was buried in the graveyard in 1850.

Wargrave is also the last resting place of one Thomas Day, author, who believed in a Rousseau-inspired creed that both people and animals could be improved by kind treatment. Having failed to train a poor orphan girl to be his dutiful wife he reared a foal that no one else was allowed to touch. On 28 September 1789 the same animal, by now an adult horse, kicked him to death at Boar Hill above Wargrave.

Walking through Shiplake

The Thames Path stays on the northern bank all the way from Sonning to Henley, but takes a detour away from the river to pass through Shiplake. There are no ships here but the lake was a dip for sheep, hence the original name of Sheeplake. The valley begins to close again after the Loddon delta and chalky eminences rise on both sides. The river has cut hard against the Berkshire bank, which is a steep tree-mottled scarp, but has treated the Oxfordshire side more gently. Although the boundary of the Chilterns' Area of Outstanding Natural Beauty descends close to the river it fails to cross it and embrace the more dramatic landscape which forms the eastern backdrop for Henley.

Alfred, Lord Tennyson married Emily Sellwood here on 13 June 1850, in the same year that he became Poet Laureate, and Eric Blair (who wrote under the name of George Orwell) stayed for a while in the twentieth century.

On the wooded chalk hillside between Remenham and Wargrave, opposite Shiplake, is a narrow valley with close-mown lawns spilling down to the water's edge. This is Happy Valley, crossed by the A321 on a very unhappy narrow hump-backed bridge which has been the scene of many traffic accidents. The bridge, victor of most duels with motor vehicles, is built of huge irregular stones said to have been taken from Reading Abbey. The habit of taking stones from sacred places seems to have reached epidemic proportions at Park Place, the former estate of General Henry Conway, who managed to acquire a complete megalithic circle from the island of Jersey. Conway, who just happened to be Governor of Jersey, shipped the 45 large granite stones from St Helier to London and then by Thames barge to Happy Valley. The Thames leg took a week and a number of megaliths seem to have been lost overboard but the ones that survived were re-erected as a 7.6-m (25-ft)

Henley-on-Thames, Oxfordshire

The Chiltern Hills and the River Thames at one of its finest locations combine to provide the historic market town of Henley-on-Thames with the setting it truly deserves. Meadows in public ownership, such as those seen here on the left of the photograph, lead straight into the heart of the town by the bridge. Rod Eyot, the inhabited island in the centre of the river, is frequently flooded in winter so all its houses are built on stilts.

Marsh Lock, Oxfordshire

Dignified by its tall trees, Marsh Lock is usually a popular destination for promenading visitors to Henley-on-Thames. The mixed woodland rising up the chalk escarpment on the Berkshire bank is a delight to the senses in all seasons of the year, but particularly in late autumn before the leaves fall. This photograph records the rare sight of the elevated horse towing path (now the Thames Path) being renovated by a number of working river boats. The lock house here has a series of markers on its wall recording the heights of various historic floods. The open meadow beyond is one of the loveliest parts of the Thames Path.

wide circle in the grounds of Park Place in 1788. The stones are now in the garden of Temple Combe, the only house in Britain to be designed (in 1958) by the American architect Frank Lloyd Wright.

The delights of Henley

Henley is the quintessential Thames-side town, the soul of the river in physical form. Hidden behind the façade of the Royal Regatta, which gives one image to the world, is another deeper and more satisfying place where people live and work. Here the beech woods of the chalky Chilterns come close and the town, river and woods seem squeezed together hugger-mugger. Henley is one of the few places to welcome the river and use it as an asset, with public open spaces and riverside walks on both sides leading north and south along the Thames Path. The river here flows disconcertingly against most people's innate sense of direction under the classical balustraded Henley Bridge (built in 1786), with its sculpted heads of Thames and Isis.

The old market town atmosphere still survives although the market barely does. Henley boasts the fourth oldest theatre (1805) in the country, the Kenton, and a much disputed 1930s cinema, the Regal, which is under threat of demolition at the time of writing. During the regatta the town hums with famous and partying people and American rowing crews, looking like Arnold Schwarzenegger clones, stalk the streets in rowing formation. Henley and environs also has its fair share of well-known residents, including ex-Beatle George Harrison, playwright John Mortimer and the actors Jeremy Irons and George Cole.

The first Oxford-Cambridge boat race was rowed at Henley on 10 June 1829 and attracted a crowd of 20,000. The regatta itself was seen as a money-spinner for the town and was devised at a public meeting in the Town Hall on 26 March 1839. But Henley Regatta was devised for only 'the right sort' of amateur rowers. As the Henley rules got more complicated to keep out the other rowers, disputes between the amateurs became divided by class. The Amateur Rowing Association (ARA) excluded members who were 'engaged in a menial duty' and in 1919 George V was very annoyed when a crew of First World War servicemen were not allowed on the water for a peace regatta. American actress Grace Kelly's father, an Olympic Gold, was excluded in 1920 and in 1936 the entire Australian Olympic crew were refused entry because they were policemen and considered to be manual workers. It's all different today, of course.

Henley Royal Regatta, Oxfordshire

During the first week of July each year Henley-on-Thames hosts an enormous summer party. A lot of people sail to the regatta by boat but, as can be seen in the photograph, more arrive by car. A race is in progress here, with the umpire's boat observing at the rear. All other river traffic is herded off the course by white booms and upright posts, and avidly monitored by the river police boats.

Brakspears provides one of Henley's liquid treasures and the brewery still hangs up the traditional switches of holly and mistletoe in its yard to ensure prosperity and good luck. On the riverside is a boathouse topped with a giant bee, the Brakspears' emblem.

South of Henley, Marsh Lock and the meadow beyond, with its cast iron sunken marker bollards, are a tranquil world apart. Northwards in Fawley Meadows stands Fawley Court, built by Sir Christopher Wren in 1684. Grinling Gibbons did the woodwork and Capability Brown landscaped the grounds in 1770.

The Thames Path crosses Henley Bridge and follows the whole length of the regatta course – except during the regatta itself, when the towpath is legally closed to accommodate the exclusive stewards and public enclosures. Temple Island marks the start of the regatta and a magnificent sweep of the river past Greenlands and Mill End to Aston.

The Hambledon Valley

After Hambledon Lock the Thames Path follows the ferry road up to the wonderfully named Flower Pot Hotel before going up and across the grounds of Culham Court, which was built in 1770. Over the river lies Greenlands, once the home of W H Smith who was famous as a bookseller but less so as Viscount Hambledon, First Lord of the Admiralty, MP and early supporter of England's oldest environmental body, The Commons Preservation Society. In the Chilterns above Greenlands Lord MacAlpine keeps his train set, although he uses the real thing. Cyclists on quiet Chiltern byways have sometimes had to dismount to allow lowloaders bearing steam engines to pass by.

Hambledon Mill, which can be approached by a short detour over the weir, was a working mill on the river until 1957. Now it is subdivided into flats, which oversee the annual battles of Hambledon Lock when hundreds of champagne bargees attempt to pass through the eye of a needle on their way to Henley Regatta. It has become quite a spectator sport. A pleasant walkway over the weir joins the recreational footpaths of the Hambledon Valley to the Henley Reach and the Thames Path. Mill End was favoured by the Romans for villas, and some say there is a poltergeist in the manor house. From the manor house an ancient yew walk points

Hambledon Mill, Buckinghamshire

After the straight regatta course the Thames curls back on itself, in a wide graceful arc, to Hambledon Lock. The Thames Path follows the Berkshire bank and is popular with local walkers. A minor detour off the path over Hambledon Lock gates leads across the weir system to the white-painted mill, which has now been converted into private flats. In the top right-hand corner of the photograph is the Italianate house Greenlands, home in the nineteenth century to W H Smith, the book magnate.

towards a tree-girt pond that recently had to be exorcised to bring an end to some spooky happenings.

The Hambledon Valley and its main village are of film-set quality and so just about every film crew in the western hemisphere has spent time there working on films from *Chitty Chitty Bang Bang* to *Paradise Postponed*. Getting to the village shop can be tricky unless you happen to be dressed in period clothes.

Swan-upping along the Thames

In the charm of the valley between Hambledon and Hurley, Thames Path walkers may glimpse the iridescent dash of the kingfisher or the slow lugubrious flight of the heron. Nature and man have become reconciled to each other to a certain extent here although many species continue to decline in numbers. The population of mute swans, however, has been brought back from the brink of extinction since the use of lead weights by fishermen was stopped. The swans are important birds in the cultural background of the Thames Path: many pubs and armorial devices use them as images. The county of Buckinghamshire takes this splendid bird as its corporate logo but the most bizarre connection is surely with swan-upping.

Every year, in the third week of July, the hereditary Royal Swan Keeper is rowed up to Henley in his randan, which is a boat designed for three people. In an unbroken tradition going back 700 years and, with the keeper dressed in his full ceremonial attire, the swans are caught, examined and returned to the river. Most swans are claimed as property of the Crown but some belong to the Dyers and Vintners Companies and are marked as such with special nicks on their beaks.

The historical legacy of Hurley

A little further on from Hambledon is the gentle village of Hurley, with its tree-lined meadows and willowed eyots. The common lands of the Manor of Hurley also give another glimpse of its sense of place and a plaque records that they are in the ownership of the parish. Temple, near Hurley, is the site of a new footbridge that was built between Berkshire and Buckinghamshire in 1989. This is the first of the custom-built Thames Path bridges which have been commissioned to link sections of towpath marooned by the closure of the ferries. It was opened by Lord Hesketh on 24 May 1989 on behalf of its collaborative builders and sponsors – Thames Water,

Hambledon, Buckinghamshire

A short walk away from the Thames Path is the village of Hambledon, in its own little valley with a tinkling clear-watered stream full (when it flows) of wild watercress. A walk over the fields brings the Chilterns beech woods into close proximity. The flint and brick housing style is typical of the Chilterns but few places combine all the best ingredients of visual perfection as well as Hambledon.

the Countryside Commission, the County and Borough Councils, Hurley Parish Council, the Ramblers' Association and generous local individuals. The footbridge is a sweeping structure of concrete and wood which can make a satisfying xylophonic noise when it is crossed.

The village also boasts the Hurley Marrow Wassail, a festival held each October on St Pyr's Day and generally close to a local pub. A Marrow Queen carries the village's biggest marrow grown that year round the nearest orchard to sacrifice the 'tree bird' to ensure a good crop the following year. The tree bird is ceremonially buried, toast is hung in the tree branches and cider or beer poured on the roots.

The Glorious Revolution of 1688 (during which James II was forced to flee from England and thereby leave the throne vacant for the expectant William III and Mary II) was planned in a crypt in Hurley, in the remains of a priory dissolved by Henry VIII. One John Lovelace of Ladye Place, Hurley, was the chief plotter and a grateful William of Orange, by then king, made him Captain of the Gentlemen Pensioners for services rendered.

On the opposite side of the river to the Thames Path, and well hidden in the tranquillity of Medmenham's present state, is a stain of depravity and dissolute living from the eighteenth-century days of the Hellfire Club. In 1745, the old abbey site was leased by the notorious dilettante Sir Francis Dashwood as a brothel, and his aristocratic friends dressed up as monks and chased women in the shrubbery. Weird things were allegedly also perpetrated at the Dashwood seat at West Wycombe (now owned by the National Trust), the family mausoleum and the caves beneath West Wycombe Hill.

The old ferry at Medmenham featured in British legal history when a famous rights of way case was won in the Court of Appeal on 28 March 1899. A stone tablet by the riverside still commemorates the action won through diligent research into public use down the centuries, discovering in the process that Charles II used the ferry in 1678.

The history of Bisham

From Hurley the Thames Path travels along the Buckinghamshire side of the river but provides views of Bisham, Quarry Bank Woods and Winter Hill. Bisham has an abbey, a sports centre, a church by the river and a wild wood, all of which are

Bisham Abbey, Berkshire

By way of a change from the subtle hues and forms of the natural beauty of the Chilterns, the National Sports Centre at Bisham Abbey has green tennis courts with eye-catching crimson surrounds. Now used as a training centre for sporting excellence, the abbey buildings were formerly home to the Hoby family. Elizabeth I stayed here under the protection of the Hobys during the ascendancy of her sister, Mary Tudor.

unusual. The abbey occupies a site first used by the Knights Templar in the twelfth century and was later the only monastery restored by Henry VIII after the Dissolution. It graduated into a Tudor house given to Anne of Cleves as part of her divorce settlement from Henry, and later harboured Elizabeth I when she stayed with the Hoby family. The present occupiers are the Sports Council, which has constructed a floodlit sports centre.

Lady Elizabeth Hoby was a brilliant and eccentric scholar. Legend has it that she had a clever son Edward, a fool Thomas and a dunce William. Poor legendary Willy was incapable of writing without blotting his copy books and Lady Hoby allegedly beat him to death as a result. Her ghost is said to stalk the place (looking like a photographic negative), wringing and washing her hands in the River Thames, which also flows past in the ghostly background. Interestingly, during house repairs some blotted copy books were discovered stuffed under the floorboards. Legends often explain, but grossly embellish, real events and an alternative explanation is that Lady Hoby's ghost walks because she killed her only grandson, thus leaving the family estate to Edward's illegitimate son, Peregrine Pinkney.

All Saints Church, tomb of the Hobys, is delightfully situated and obliquely aligned to the river's edge. From the Thames Path on the opposite bank, the white stone church is seen against the backdrop of Quarry Bank Woods, green and russet in turn through the changing seasons of the beech tree. The woods on the chalk hillside have been bought by the Woodland Trust with assistance from the Countryside Commission, English Nature, Berkshire County Council and other local authorities. Prior to the great storms of 1987 and 1990 it was magnificent but has suffered great damage and is being helped to rise anew. It is thought that this is the woodland that inspired the Wild Wood in Kenneth Grahame's *Wind in the Willows*, so watch out for weasels!

Marlow, Frankenstein and the Gout Track

Like Henley, Marlow (a little way along from Bisham but on the north bank) has its own regatta and brewery (Wethereds) and is set in arguably the most beautiful stretch of Thames Valley in the chalk curves of the Chiltern Hills. It seems odd that Mary Shelley should write *Frankenstein* here while her husband was writing 'The

Bisham Church, Berkshire

The white Norman tower of the church at Bisham is rakishly angled to the river and acts as an upstream landmark for the approach to Marlow. It contains the tombs of the Hoby family, with that of Margaret Hoby from the seventeenth century being of especial interest. The Thames Path runs along the Buckinghamshire bank after crossing the river at the purpose-built footbridge at Temple near Hurley.

Revolt of Islam'. Perhaps Mary Shelley devised her work partly from the story of the Gout Track and its milestone in Marlow market place. The Cecils of Hatfield House, Hertfordshire, who suffered terrible gout, were desperate enough to take their coach to Bath for the spa waters but in the eighteenth century the rutted roads made the journey a torture. So they built their own, smoother, short cut from Hatfield through Marlow to the Bath Road turnpike at Reading. No doubt the Cecils would have considered having their brains transplanted into someone else's body, as described in *Frankenstein*, just to escape their gout-ridden corporeal torment.

William Tierney Clark built the famous suspension bridge (1831–6) that overlooks the even more famous Compleat Angler Hotel, but it is not so well known that Clark also built the suspension bridge over the Danube in Budapest.

The Thames Path route from Marlow to Cookham follows the northern bank and misses the opportunity to see the Thames Valley from Winter Hill, owned by the National Trust. At Bourne End the Thames Path will eventually be cantilevered off the existing Victorian railway bridge, which carries the Marlow branch line from Maidenhead. It will then follow the water's edge through the open National Trust meadows of Cock Marsh to Cookham. This is a deservedly popular spot for walking and sailing.

The history of Cookham

Cookham is a very old place. It has two megaliths, the Cookham Stone and the Tarry Stone, hidden away and Bronze Age barrows lying on Cock Marsh next to Cookham Common. The Romans crossed the river here on the Camlet Way from Silchester to Verulanium (St Albans). Danes and Saxon invaders used its riverside marshes and meadows and these have been assiduously preserved through time as common lands. The setting of Cookham and its restricted urban spread is due to the tenacity of commoners' rights more than the planning system. From Widbrook Common through Odney Common, Cookham Moor, Cookham Common and Cock Marsh runs unspoilt open landscape. Some is now in National Trust ownership.

The classic modern painter, Sir Stanley Spencer, hid daily scenes of Cookham's landscapes in nearly all of his pictures. He was born here, lived in the village for 49 years and had a remarkable family life. His penniless father, William, at one time owned only a dressing gown, slippers and bowler hat in which he walked the streets

Quarry Bank Woods, Berkshire

The verdant woodlands rising from the river's edge along the chalk escarpment are known as Cookham's 'Little Switzerland'. The trees suffered greatly in the 1987 and 1990 storms and a major restoration project is underway through the Woodland Trust. The Thames Path follows the bank on the left towards Bourne End where it will cross the river on a walkway cantilevered off the existing railway bridge. The colourful canoes belong to Longridge, the Scouts' boating centre.

– an image that was to reappear later in one of Spencer's unfinished religious paintings. Young Stanley went to the Slade School of Fine Art in London from 1908 until 1912 but was much teased by his fellow students because he commuted from Cookham each day and was very unworldly. He silenced them by winning the composition prize with his *Apple Gatherers*, about which he wrote 'places in Cookham seem to be possessed of a sacred presence of which the inhabitants are not aware'. There is now a Stanley Spencer Gallery here in the old chapel.

Spencer's First World War experiences are captured in his greatest commission (for Burghclere Chapel), and even in this frieze of soldierly scenes parts of Cookham and Hedsor appear. In 1927 he caused a sensation because *Cookham Resurrection* featured naked bits of his wife Hilda. In the 1930s he became obsessed with another woman, Patricia Preece, so divorced his wife. He hoped to retain the sexual attentions of both women but failed. Like his father he mellowed into old age and eccentricity, pushing his paints in a pram around Cookham and turning up at his investiture in 1957 with a present for the Queen Mother in a shopping bag.

The path to Maidenhead

A less flamboyant figure, Kenneth Grahame, lived in nearby Cookham Dene and there wrote *The Wind in the Willows* to please his son Alastair. Poor little Mouse, as he was nicknamed, was blind in one eye and had a squint in the other, and passed from a sad childhood at Rugby School to a miserable adolescence at Eton and Christ Church, Oxford. He was killed by a train in 1920.

The Thames Path wobbles away from the river's braided channels at Hedsor and is set back just enough to admire nature's artwork in the steeply hanging woods below Cliveden House and grounds. Slightly higher than Taplow Court stands Cliveden House, where sexual scandal once more links people and place. In the grounds of the mansion designed by Charles Barry is a riverside cottage used by Stephen Ward and Christine Keeler in the early 1960s. It was at the Astor family's Cliveden swimming pool that John Profumo (Secretary of State for War) encountered Miss Keeler's physical charms on the night of 8 July 1961. The same physique later attracted Captain Ivanov, the Soviet Naval Attaché, and they both became her lovers. As this was during the Cold War there was a prurient scandal and tragedy subsequently visited the lives of all participants.

Cookham, Berkshire

Cookham is an ancient crossing point of the river that was certainly used by the Romans, and the Norman church was built in 1140 on Saxon foundations. The modern bridge was constructed in 1867 in iron and is pretty in its coat of white paint. 'Pretty but busy' sums up Cookham, although in the 1920s and 1930s when the artist Stanley Spencer lived here, it was much more rural. Each July the royal swan keeper starts his annual journey to mark the swans from Turk's boathouse next to the bridge.

Cliveden was different in the 1930s when the so-called Cliveden set, led by the Astors but including Joachim von Ribbentrop (German Ambassador) and Geoffrey Dawson (Editor of *The Times*), were accused by Claud Cockburn in 1936 of supporting military appeasement with Nazi Germany. That this should be so in the place where 'Rule Britannia' was performed for the first time in 1740 is one of history's little ironies.

Boulter's Lock and Taplow Court, not far from each other, had contrasting river heroes in Edwardian England. W H Turner the lock keeper and his bull terrier Juggins guided thousands of craft through the narrow lock and also controlled thousands more carried round it by muscular young men up from London for the opportunity of a tip. Turner's skills as a naval gunnery officer and cutlass instructor never had as much use as his diplomacy, packing and life-saving abilities. Sometimes he worked more than 100 hours a week. In 25 years at the lock the whole range of Victorian and Edwardian society was squeezed through this narrow gap like human toothpaste.

Up on the hill above the river at Taplow Court lived another active character – William Grenfell, who became Lord Desborough and later Chairman of the Thames Conservancy. Grenfell was an accomplished amateur athlete who climbed the Matterhorn three times, swam the Niagara rapids twice, rowed across the Channel and later became the Thames punting champion.

Domesday called Maidenhead Elentone (Ellen's Town), but it became Maidenhythe from around 1296, meaning 'maidens' landing place'. It is an ancient site and probably associated with a river crossing, although the first bridge was not built until much later. A prehistoric megalith still stands hidden in the graveyard of St Mark's Church and may once have formed a line with others in nearby Cookham.

Maidenhead currently has the world's longest single-span, brick arch bridge – the immensely satisfying railway crossing designed and built by Isambard Kingdom Brunel in 1838 for the Great Western Railway. J M W Turner may have used this bridge in his painting *Rain, Steam and Speed*, although another viaduct closer to London now seems to be the more probable location.

During the Edwardian era steamboats plied the Thames, carrying thousands of day trippers who had travelled down on the railway from London, and it is said that some of these outings ended rather disreputably. The sheer youthful exuberance of Edwardian river pleasure seeking can still be witnessed in the 1895 painting of Maidenhead's Boulter's Lock by E J Gregory.

Cliveden, Buckinghamshire

Cliveden Reach is where the floodplain woodland of Berkshire almost crosses the river to touch the Chilterns woodlands on the Hedsor to Taplow escarpment. Whether viewed from the Thames Path or the river, the trees tower on all sides and the river whispers gently under their boughs. Cliveden, once home to the Astor family but now owned by the National Trust, is perched atop the precipitous slope. The woods continue into the celebrated Burnham Beeches north-west of Slough.

The approach to Windsor Castle

The Maidenhead section of the Thames Path is prettily suburban, although it attracts many visitors in the summer. The tree-filled eyots set off well the splendid road bridge and white-painted hotels. The path crosses the bridge and marches towards Windsor past Bray, famous for its vicar, and the temporary disturbance of the M4 motorway. A small piece of Buckinghamshire squeezes down to the river here between Maidenhead and Slough and subscribes the flat infertile gravels of Dorney and Boveney.

Boveney is a truly hide-and-seek hamlet under the visual protection of Windsor Castle. The simple rustic church of St Mary Magdalen is its secret gem, possibly built on a pre-Christian sacred site with now just the river for company. It can only be reached by towpath or footpath.

Nearby Monkey Island, some say, derives its name from bizarre frescoes of monkeys dressed in eighteenth-century attire which were commissioned by the Duke of Marlborough in 1744. Others say it's a corruption of Monk's Eyot. Stirling Moss, the racing driver, once lived next to the ferry in a house called The Long White Cloud, which is where Sir Edward Elgar composed his violin concerto.

Britain's first pineapple was cultivated by John Rose in the grounds of Dorney Court in 1665 and was given to Charles II. The house is cuddled up next to the little church of St James, and they look cosy together in the huge surrounding expanse of Dorney Common and Thames Field. Open landscapes are rare today in southern England and cattle-grazed ones using commoners' rights even more so. Here tradition is strong and cows graze freely almost to the Thames. Look for the bumble bees, originally called dorney bees, from which Dorney (meaning 'bumble bee island') gets its name.

The impressively jagged outline of Windsor Castle, which alters in appearance with the ever-changing shifts in light and cloud cover, is visible for many miles. It is truly the last chalky outpost of the Chilterns. Windsor Castle is a sentinel in the same sense that the Wittenham Clumps stand guard over the Chiltern Hills north of Goring. Between them the river has shared with us its most exquisite landscape treasures. From Maidenhead and Windsor downstream the river becomes more commercial, more the throbbing life-blood of the historic development of the nation state. The population pressure increases and the river becomes lined with houses like the stones cemented to the tubes of caddis fly larvae. Nature still persists though and swallows and house martins swoop and squeal in the air all summer long, joyfully scooping up the lightly skimming midges.

Dorney Common, Buckinghamshire

A landscape of two contrasting uses is visible at Dorney; intensive geometric market gardening in the foreground and wilder open grazings cut by unfenced roads reaching towards the Thames in the distance. This flat apron of sands and silt between Maidenhead and Slough is ideal for growing market produce. Such agricultural land use is diametrically opposed to the survival of Dorney Common as a working landscape with commoner's cattle grazing right to the Thames Path.

Dorney Court, Buckinghamshire

On misty days it is not difficult to imagine medieval cowherds tending their cattle on Dorney Common, and nearby Dorney Court enhances the manorial atmosphere of this special place. The immaculately landscaped old gardens of the Tudor house, built in 1500, blend smoothly with the curtilage of the church, which in turn follows the seamless architectural quality of the manor house. The Palmer family have lived here for over 400 years and Britain's first pineapple was grown in the grounds by one John Rose. His achievement is commemorated in the name of the local pub, The Pineapple. Anyone willing to be tempted in the summer may find the short detour along the footpath to Dorney Court is rewarded by a cream tea.

Royal Thames

The shapes, sizes and rulers of royal tribal territories have repeatedly changed throughout the occupation of the Thames Valley by settled peoples, but there have been two great riverside markers to royal continuity: Windsor Castle and Hampton Court. Windsor Castle remains because of the wealth of solid building material on and around the mound where William the Conqueror placed his military stronghold in the eleventh century. Its strategic command of the river suggests that the site is much older. Hampton Court was the scene of a royal clash, when the human frailties of Henry VIII and Cardinal Wolsey met spectacularly over Henry's belief in the divine right of kings and his desire to divorce his first wife, Catherine of Aragon. The river that bore Wolsey to his subsequent execution, and later Henry's corpse to Windsor, was once thick with royal barges and rivermen plying their trade in the way taxis do today. The section between Windsor and Kingston, a royal town and crowning point of many Anglo-Saxon kings, is now much overgrown with suburban dwellings and riverside villas peeping through curtains of weeping willow. Water abounds: in all directions lie either gravel-extracted lagoons or the embanked containers for London's potable water supply. These twentieth-century reservoirs, lying under the flight paths around Heathrow, nearly all bear the names of royal kings or queens.

Windsor Castle is Berkshire's most internationally famous landmark and has grown from a mound in William the Conqueror's time, through work ordered by Henry II, Edward III, Elizabeth I and later additions from other monarchs, into the world's largest inhabited castle. It played host to the earliest meetings of the Order of the Garter when, in 1346, it was supposed that the fallen garter of Joan, Countess of Salisbury, was picked up and worn by Edward III on his leg while he said 'Honi soit qui mal y pense' (evil be to him who evil thinks) to the assembled Court. The secret

Windsor, Berkshire

There can be no doubting the claim that Windsor Castle is one of the world's greatest buildings. Its dominant position is equally impressive and based on military principles. The Thames Path skirts the edge of the open space beneath the castle which is called Home Park and used for the Windsor Horse Show and other public events. The long strip of woodland in the middle of the river is called the Cobler and the towing path used to run along it from Romney Lock to Windsor Bridge

behind the affair is rather peculiar – for a start, Joan was not the Countess of Salisbury but Edward I's grand-daughter, the 'Fair Maid of Kent'. She was betrothed to the Earl of Salisbury but while he was fighting the French Wars she became involved with Thomas Holland. Salisbury returned but Joan married Holland instead in 1348. In 1346, however, Joan, who was an active teenage beauty of some repute, may have been a member of a witches' coven to which Edward III also belonged; the blue garter was its emblem. Losing such an article in front of others could have had dire consequences but for Edward's firm warning. Joan later married Edward III's son, the Black Prince (after she was widowed at 32), and subsequently became the mother of Richard II.

Elizabeth I extended the castle and built the North Terrace with its superb views of the river. She also told William Shakespeare to write her a funny play, and had the resulting *Merry Wives of Windsor* performed at the castle in 1593.

Sir Christopher Wren was not short of a merry jape or two either, and when charged with building the Town Hall in 1690 he constructed the ground floor with all four internal 'supporting' pillars 5 cm (2 in) short of the ceiling. Such cosmetic fun would not be right for St George's Chapel, inside the castle walls, which is arguably the finest Perpendicular building in Britain. However, it is the Round Tower that commands the mound and has views over 12 counties (subject to local government reorganization). Queen Victoria completed the extensive modernization that had begun in 1824 and eventually cost more than £1 million. She is buried with Albert in nearby Home Park.

The castle's setting on a chalky prominence above the river is no less spectacular on its dip slope, where the huge expanse of Windsor Great Park and the old Forest of Windsor spread out southwards. The vista is divided by avenues of trees and rides aligned to landmarks or statuary. The broadness of the rides was necessary to allow kings like Georges III and IV to follow the stag-hunting hounds in their carriages.

One of the most mysterious events at Windsor took place on 18 August 1783 and was witnessed from the Terrace by the artist Thomas Sandby and several eminent scientists. The Royal Society's eye witness report records that a moving, brilliantly lit, spherical object under an oblong cloud halted in the sky, changed colour, direction and shape, split into two small bodies and disappeared with an explosion. Sandby recreated the scene in aquatint and a copy, housed in the British Museum, is thought to be of the world's first watercolour of a UFO.

The traditions of Eton

Eton is joined almost seamlessly to Windsor by the marvellous pedestrianized bridge that spans the Thames here. There is a time-warp strangeness to Eton and a tendency for outsiders to gawp at the anachronistic dress of its school boys. The oddest thing about the World's Most Famous Public School is that it was originally intended (in 1440) to educate 24 poor and indigent scholars.

Hidden behind various walls are a number of playing fields; some are just called The Playing Fields but others delight in weird names like Agars Plough and The Brocas. The Wall Game is equally bizarre and its rules are quite impenetrable. Eton

College is now well known for rowing, but before 1840 the boys were forbidden to go on the river. To get round this 'shirking' was introduced – boys who were rowing covered their faces with a raised arm when stopped by unjolly masters. This meant that they admitted they were being naughty but the masters had to pretend they couldn't see them.

When leaving Windsor and Eton, security reasons dictate that the Thames Path crosses Victoria Bridge to the opposite side of the river below the royal apartments and Home Park before rejoining the Berkshire bank at Albert Bridge. Two new sections of path will be created to make this link through Datchet.

Datchet, an unusual bridge and Old Windsor

Datchet itself is a real river village with royal connections, mainly because the highway from London crossed the river there, first as a ferry from 1249 to 1706 and thereafter by bridge. However, bridge building was not without its problems and George III had to supply a free ferry between 1795 and 1811 when the wooden bridge became unsafe. The Crown used legal duress to insist that a bridge be constructed by the counties of Berkshire and Buckinghamshire but, whether out of spite or sheer incompetence, Buckinghamshire built its bit out of wood and Berkshire its half out of iron.

Datchet Mead was the setting for a scene in Shakespeare's *The Merry Wives of Windsor*, in which Falstaff was 'carried in a basket like a barrow of butcher's offal' and dumped in the river.

Residents of Datchet may not realize it but Leigh House had a cats' cemetery in its grounds where Lady Cholmondeley interred more than 30 cats (each with a coffin and gravestone) and made a provision in her will to ensure they were not disturbed. Today the graves (but not the stones) are in the middle of a housing estate and are still undisturbed.

The Thames Path slips alongside New Cut to Old Windsor, where William the Conqueror left Edward the Confessor's Anglo-Saxon wooden palace by the riverside to build a stronger castle of stone, but the riverside church, which still stands, is of Norman origin. The churchyard contains the forgotten grave of Mary Robinson, a beautiful actress of the eighteenth century who was called 'Fair Perdita' after her success in that role in *The Winter's Tale*. For a time in 1779 the Prince Regent (and future George IV) made her his mistress. This resourceful and talented woman died in poverty in 1800 at the age of 42. Perhaps guided by a peculiar sense of Hanoverian irony, one of the first Nazi V2 rockets to hit Britain fell on Old Windsor in September 1944, near the Bells of Ouzely public house. Its curious name is said to derive from Henry VIII's time when some Oxford monks, who were fleeing the Dissolution on rafts (plus monastery bells), came to grief at Old Windsor and hid their precious bells in the river silt (or ooze).

Behind Old Windsor lies the Royal Forest of Windsor and Windsor Great Park – immense landscapes of outstanding interest and variety with ancient oaks looking like stumpy candles reduced to rivulets of lumpy wax. Most of the old forest areas, although interplanted with more recently sown trees, have been designated as Sites

Eton, Berkshire

At the heart of the village of Eton is the world famous public school, although it is rarely regarded in its landscape setting from this perspective. Around the fifteenth-century college, chapel and cloisters, which form the nucleus of this photograph, the playing fields and open spaces of The Brocas can be seen by the Thames. The school's green club carries out environmental improvements alongside the river when the pupils are not studying or in training for the Eton Wall Game. Eton High Street links the Thames Path to the college chapel and has some interesting shops. When the boating weather is jolly this is the place to be.

of Special Scientific Interest. Herne the Hunter met his end in this forest and his ghost may dance with that of Sir Charles Augustus Murray, buried at Old Windsor, a man with the unique distinction of having given London Zoo its first hippopotamus.

Runnymede and Magna Carta

Although on the opposite (northern) side of the river to that expected, Wraysbury is a Saxon Berkshire settlement. This is the parish that gave the world Magna Carta, although all of the pomp is celebrated on the southern (Surrey) side at Runnymede. Magna Carta island is believed, possibly erroneously, to be the actual place where the Great Charter was signed on 19 June 1215, but it is no longer an island. The house built there contains a stone tablet which was dredged from the river in the nineteenth century and is reputed to be the writing table on which King John signed and sealed the baron's demands and also the Charta de Foresta. Nobody knows for sure whether or not John met the mob here but it is perhaps interesting to consider where you would have strategically placed yourself as King John: in the same field as 15–30,000 antagonistic soldiers or (protected only by a small force of mercenaries) on the opposite side of a large river close to the hospitality of a Benedictine nunnery. The charter might well have been negotiated with the barons on Runnymede, but the petitioning, and therefore legally inferior party, would have to come across the river by boat to have it signed.

Certainty in such matters is impossible but it is a fact that the nunnery existed and it was on an island in the ownership of the Ankerwyke Nunnery that Magna Carta was signed under a large tree. The tumbled ruins of the nunnery now barely exist and are hidden among the woods, ponds and ditches of the site. Ankerwyke also has a massive yew tree, badly damaged by the 1987 hurricane, that was said by Dr Lardener in the sixteenth-century *Arboretum Britannicum* to be 2000 years old. Was this the big tree under which Magna Carta was signed? Henry VIII later wooed Anne Boleyn under its boughs and later still, so legend says, waited there for the signal that her execution had been carried out at Tower Hill (despite the fact that he was in Wiltshire at the time).

The land by the river was formerly the site of the picnic, the landing stage and thatched house mentioned in *Three Men in a Boat*. The box hedges of its garden can still be found but the house has long gone. The Ankerwyke Estate is now owned by Berkshire County Council and a major effort is underway to conserve this secretive place in conjunction with English Heritage. A breeding colony of shrieking escaped parakeets now mock all this history.

At Runnymede on the south bank of the river, through which the Thames Path runs, American memorabilia is taking over; 0.4 hectare (1 acre) here was given to the American people for the John F Kennedy memorial and adjacent to it is the gift of the American Bar Association, a sort of temple gazebo. The impressive-looking gateposts and lodges are nothing to do with Magna Carta either but were designed by Sir Edwin Lutyens to commemorate Urban Broughton (Lord Fairhaven, who owned the land and gave it to the National Trust) in 1929.

Staines and the urban Thames

Slightly downriver from Runnymede is Staines, a town whose modern appearance belies a fascinating historical importance. The name derives from 'stana', the Anglo-Saxon for stone; the Romans called it Pontes after its bridges. It is likely that a Celtic trackway crossed the river here, but both track and crossing were turned into a new Roman road and bridge from London to Silchester around AD 43. Staines marked the Thames' most important boundary, the upper limit of its tidal reach before man-made constructions were used to impede its flow. There is still a stone at Staines and it is intimately connected with the tides and the City of London. The London Stone, as it is called, sits on a plinth in the recreation ground above Staines Bridge and states 'God Preserve ye Citty of London'. It is old but probably later than the date carved on it of 1285. Commercial control of the river below the London Stone was jealously held by the City and an annual river inspection made its way downstream to restate the rights. The Lord Mayor 'bumped' new aldermen on the stone on these inspections, and for a fee they would be made Free Watermen of the River Thames.

Staines adds increasingly to the urban texture of the Thames Path hinterland although countryside still intrudes strongly around Penton Hook and Laleham.

The naturally formed ox-bow bend in the river at Penton Hook has been much abused by human interference over the years. It is surrounded by wet gravel pits, a theme park, marina and a lock/weir system. Laleham Abbey is not far away and the tomb of Matthew Arnold, the nineteenth-century poet and critic who was born in Laleham, lies in the wooded churchyard. In 1770 the Thames here was only 1.3 m (4 ft) deep at Laleham ferry point and cattle were made to swim the river over to Chertsey Meads.

Nearby, and completely hidden because no trace of it can be found, is Chertsey Abbey, once one of the greatest abbeys in England and built in 666. It was completely shattered during the Reformation and not a stone remains, although parts of it were incorporated into Hampton Court. The Thames has been a great highway for stones, not only after the Reformation but also after the Great Fire of London in 1666 when rubble was dumped on eyots upstream and stone from Oxfordshire and Berkshire was shipped to London.

After Chertsey Meads the river crashes into 'plotland', where bungalows cling to the river's edge with the tenacious grip of freshwater limpets. The River Wey, the Wey Navigation (a canal wholly owned by the National Trust) and the Thames all meet in a mass of houses, islands, locks and weirs.

St George's Hill at Weybridge, which now epitomizes the conspicuously wealthy end of suburban housing, has been in turn a Celtic and Roman camp and, irony of ironies, an encampment for the Diggers, an offshoot of Cromwell's Commonwealth, who tilled the land together as a co-operative venture.

Opposite Shepperton the Countryside Commission will have to order the construction of a new footbridge, taking the Thames Path over to the southern side of the Desborough Cut to replace the long-lost ferry service. The path heads for Walton-on-Thames, Sunbury-on-Thames, Hampton and Taggs Island, with suburban housing and bungalows filling nearly every space on both sides of the river.

Coway Stakes, now a park near Walton Bridge at Walton, is derived from 'causeway stakes' after the lines of huge stakes that the Venerable Bede, the seventh-century historian and scholar, saw here. Romantics will believe that they were part of Caesar's battle with Cassivelaunus in 54 BC, but sceptics think they were fish traps. They have not been seen now for more than a century.

Walton Church has a replica of a scold's bridle hidden away and a giant tomb to Viscount Shannan which is anything but hidden. Louis François Roubiliac was commissioned by Lady Middlesex to sculpt it in the 1740s but this hideous carbuncle was the source of much complaint from the congregation because it blocked out the light. Canaletto came to paint the old bridge in the 1750s. The landscape was almost entirely rural then, with only distant pockets of housing clustered around parish churches.

Bronze and Iron Age settlements have been discovered at Sunbury-on-Thames and Cloven Barrow, a Bronze Age burial mound, is still visible. Sunbury was a Domesday village that became fashionable with wealthy merchants from London in the 1660s. Platt's Eyot has been the home of Thorneycroft's torpedo boats, although you are unlikely to meet one on active military service on the river today as most of them disappeared after the Battle of Jutland in 1916.

Not much further downstream is Hampton. David Garrick, the famous eighteenth-century actor and theatre manager, came here in 1754 and a village peopled by admirers grew up around him. His features live on in stone in Roubiliac's bust of Shakespeare in Garrick's Temple by the riverside at Hampton House. A few steps further down the Thames Path will lead walkers to Taggs Island. Fred Karno, famous for his circus, made the island an entertainment centre although all that is left now is a real Swiss chalet transported from Switzerland in 1899. There are no remains either of *The Satsuma* and *The Astoria*, two battleship-sized double-decker houseboats that were built on the island.

The splendours of Hampton Court

Although not exactly the most hidden expanse of Thames-side scenery, nonetheless Hampton Court, which lies a little way downstream from Hampton, has its share of secrets. For instance, Hampton Court Bridge is built of camouflaged concrete. It was designed by Sir Edwin Lutyens and erected in 1933, yet looks like something from a much earlier era in mellow bricks and Portland stone.

Penton Hook, Surrey

The natural tendency of the Thames to form meanders and ox-bow curves when crossing homogenously soft geology is well illustrated at Penton Hook. Penton Hook Island is almost Amazonian compared with its fringe of chalets, bungalows, mobile home parks and marinas. This is a transition zone between countryside and urban areas. The Thames Path follows the lock-side track in the foreground and in the distance is the rising ground of the North Downs.

Hampton Court Park and Palace, Middlesex

The full splendour of Hampton Court and its powerful setting in the great loop of the Thames is captured in this photograph. The architectural work of Sir Christopher Wren is masterfully blended with the original Elizabethan design. The Great Gatehouse, with its oriel window and the arms of Henry VIII, leads into the Base Court and, opposite, directly to Anne Boleyn's Gateway. Here, in turn, another gateway leads into the Clock Court where Nicholas Oursian's wonderful Astronomical Clock of 1540 can be admired. Beyond the buildings the landscape is equally dramatic, with topiary and yew-walks leading to long avenues and vast triangles formed by water courses. The town of Kingston-upon-Thames sprawls across the horizon.

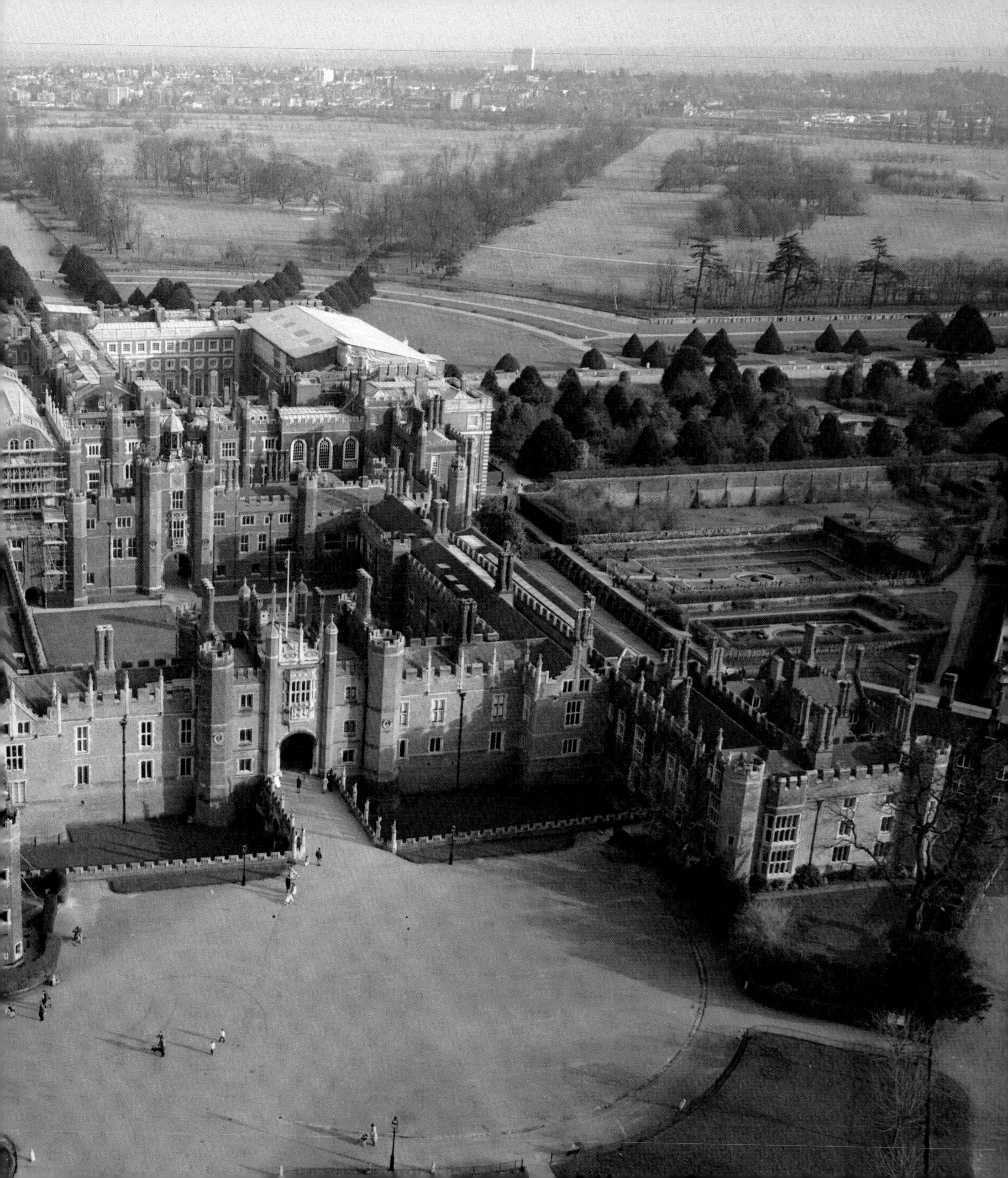

Hampton Court Palace bears little resemblance to the butcher's shop in Ipswich in which its first owner, Cardinal Wolsey, spent his early years. The Palace still exudes misplaced power and dominance (with later additions by Henry VIII and William and Mary) and contains 1000 rooms. Three thousand individual weapons are on display in the King's Guardroom and, for those who prefer gentler fun, the ceiling paintings on the King's Staircase by Verrio feature the faces of all the parlour maids he bedded during his stay. It would take three days to visit all the rooms in the palace. There is the haunted gallery (naturally), in which Catherine Howard has walked since her execution for adultery in 1542 (Henry VIII found it quicker and less messy than divorce).

Charles I's collection of Renaissance art is housed in the Lower Orangery. He spent £10,500 in 1629, then a truly staggering sum of money, to buy the Duke of Mantua's art collection, including Raphael's Cartoons. The popular conception of the time was that this action was so bizarre as to be worthy of derision – from which the modern use of the word 'cartoon' has sprung.

On the exterior of the palace is the Astronomical Clock built by Nicholas Oursian for Henry VIII in 1540, which also tells the time of high water at London Bridge, and the Great Vine which was planted in 1768 and is still thriving. Other features include the famous maze (1714) and Henry VIII's real tennis courts – the oldest in the world but now superceded by modern ones. There are one or two lawns here too – Bushy Park and Hampton Park together occupy more than 800 hectares (2000) acres. William of Orange was very keen to outshine the splendours of Versailles and his attempt was impressive.

The Thames Path follows the full length of the south side of the park to Kingston-upon-Thames and walkers will doubtless become connoisseurs of brickwork as they walk along it.

An ancient crowning place

The Royal Borough of Kingston, as the name suggests, has an association with kings and the name derives from Cyninges-tun (a Celtic Kings' Manor). It became a favoured crowning place for Anglo-Saxon kings, like Ethelred the Unready in 979, because of its stone of investiture (which still stands and can be seen near the Guildhall). The sanctity of stones is a recurrent theme along the Thames from the source to the Stone of Destiny, which sits beneath the Coronation Chair in

Hampton Court, Middlesex

The red Tudor brickwork of Hampton Court Palace is positively crimson in certain lights, as in this photograph; indeed, by all accounts, as red as Henry VIII's beard and as fiery as his temper. It was partly Henry's displeasure with Cardinal Wolsey for this building's ostentatious and challenging display of wealth and power that led to the latter's execution. Seen here is the moat bridge lined with carvings of the royal beasts: the White Greyhound of Richmond, the Yale of Beaufort, the Red Dragon of Wales, the Unicorn of Scotland, the Lion of England and five other animals.

Westminster Abbey. This coronation stone was believed to have such potency that Edward I ordered it to be sent from Scone in Scotland in 1297. Some stones allegedly had the ability to shriek or roar when a true king stood on them barefoot. Sitting or standing on such stones obviously has some echo of the prehistoric belief in making contact with *genius loci*, the spirit of sacred places. The Roman method of founding new towns by augury and setting down a sacred omphalos, or stone, works on the same principle. Indeed, another Thames stone not to be missed is the London Stone, now set into a wall in Cannon Street but at one time possibly the omphalos of Roman Londinium. Dramatic events were declared on it and its authority was recognized. Even Jack Cade, the Irish leader of the insurrection against Henry VI, hit it with his sword in 1450 as a challenge from the rebels to the citizens of London.

Kingston also has an ancient right to hold markets, which is partly due to the fordable nature of the river here, the lowest point downstream where livestock could cross safely. The Guildhall Market has existed for 700 years.

At Kingston-upon-Thames the Thames Path becomes a twin track route and follows, wherever possible, both sides of the river. It is possible to cross each road bridge so that walkers can add a variety of perspectives to their enjoyment. It is here that the Thames matures and becomes London's river.

The final approach to London

The density of housing and buildings crowds in close at times, as at Teddington and Twickenham, or suddenly and unexpectedly retreats to a far-off shoreline, leaving a deserted grassy strand. All rugby fans who know Twickenham as Twickers are close to the hidden fact that the name means 'Twicca's dry ground'. Dry or not, it is world-famous as the home of England's international rugby matches. Alfred, Lord Tennyson, J M W Turner and Sir Francis Bacon all lived here, as did Alexander Pope who also spent some time further upriver at Stanton Harcourt. Britain's first weeping willow was planted here in 1730 and is now one of the Thames' most common suburban trees.

The monument to mark the dividing line between the Port of London Authority and the former Thames Water Authority stands nearby. Now the Thames is administered by the National Rivers Authority which keeps watch over the privatized activities of its former colleagues in Thames Water.

The waterfront of Twickenham is perhaps best known for Eel Pie Island, which is linked by a footbridge to the passing route of the Thames Path. Eel Pie Island was

Isleworth, London

There can be no greater contrast to the power of Hampton Court Park's landscape than this view of the allotments behind Isleworth churchyard. Here too is the creative power of man to dig, to grow, to experience peace and gentle satisfaction in the simple pleasures of allotment gardening – this is the living link with the medieval manorial strip system of agriculture. The Thames Path leaves the riverside here to veer past the church into Syon Park.

once just a tree-covered eyot popular for picnics, although it later became a jazz club and rock and roll venue favoured by those seeking the joint attractions of riverside riffs and the young Rolling Stones. You would not know it now and it is doubtful whether any archaeologists of the future would discover its secrets.

A note on eel pies is required here. The *Cook's Oracle* of 1843 reports that an eel pie is made from eels, parsley, sherry, shallots, butter and lemon and covered in puff pastry. When people had time to debate such matters on Richmond Hill the vital question was whether to eat the pies hot or cold. There is still a local pub which bears the name The Eel Pie, but sadly the tradition of serving eel pies in riverside hostelries has died out completely.

After Eel Pie Island the river and the Thames Path move through two open parklands – Marble Hill to the north and Petersham Meadows to the south. The house in Marble Hill Park was built by George II to house his mistress Henrietta Howard, the Countess of Suffolk. Henrietta was but one of George's mistresses but the Palladian mansion and parkland were of truly royal proportions. Alexander Pope laid out the park's design and Britain's largest black walnut tree grows there.

Across the river to the south, if the seasonally regulated ferry is running, are Ham House and Petersham Meadows. Ham House was the seventeenth-century powerbase of the Duke and Duchess of Lauderdale. It is now owned by the National Trust, as are Petersham Meadows, one of the very first landscape preservation efforts of the young Octavia Hill and the Kyrle Society, who were 'dedicated to placing objects of beauty within reach of the poor'. Octavia became one of the three founders of the National Trust on 16 July 1894. Petersham Church is worth a visit for the feel of its eighteenth-century interior and the grave of George Vancouver, explorer of Canada and after whom Vancouver Island is named.

An old palace and the view from Richmond Hill

Petersham Meadows lie at the foot of the terrace on Richmond Hill and were preserved because of the inspirational view from the top. The Thames winds round from Kingston and reflects the setting sun through a multiple layered screen of trees. The town of Richmond was given its name by Henry VII, who also held the Earldom of Richmond, North Yorkshire. It was formerly called Schene or Sheen ('shining' or 'beautiful') and, despite the ravages of traffic and congestion, it is still one of the most enchanting of London's riverside villages. Old Palace, the original royal residence, is nearly all gone. Richard II had it pulled down after his wife, Anne of Bohemia, died from plague in 1394 and it was from the rebuilt palace that Henry VIII, in his envy of Cardinal Wolsey, hopped over to Hampton Court. Elizabeth I slept here as a prisoner of her sister Mary and much later died here. The only part that remains is the gatehouse, which still bears Henry VIII's coat of arms. Richmond Green was once a jousting yard.

The Georgian buildings of Richmond are still impressive as they tread up Richmond Hill from the river towards the vast Royal Park. Richmond Hill Terrace is a magnificent viewpoint of the looping Thames that has inspired poets, writers and artists for centuries, including Charles Dickens, J M W Turner, Sir Joshua Reynolds,

Vincent Van Gogh and Sir Walter Scott. Detouring Thames Path walkers standing here will be able to admire the view, catch their breath, gaze down on Petersham Meadows and visually retrace their steps.

Not much further along the hill, the bulk of the Star and Garter Home partially obscures the entrance to Richmond Park which, in Charles I's day, enclosed 912 hectares (2253 acres). Richmond Park is the most rural lifeline the population of London has but it was not always so accessible and lawsuits had to be applied to maintain ancient rights of way through it. Today it is a delight to spot the red and fallow deer hiding nervously among the bracken and oaks.

The intellect of William Cobbett, the eighteenth-century author of *Rural Rides*, was stirred into action in Richmond when, at the age of 11 and on his way through there to find work as a gardener at nearby Kew, he spent his last threepence on a copy of Jonathan Swift's *Tale of a Tub*. The lyrics of 'Rule Britannia' were written here and in 1876 Vincent Van Gogh, who was living in Lambeth at the time, hurled off Richmond Bridge an earring belonging to Ursula Loyer, daughter of his landlady and the subject of his unrequited affections. Until then he had worn the earring himself – in the same ear that he later hacked off.

Tidal Thames

It is difficult to think of Staines as a potential seaside town but at one time the tide lapped all the way up to a point roughly marked by the site of its London Stone. The river could be forded at low tide in several places so settlements grew at the crossing points, especially where firm gravel banks provided a platform for habitation. London may have begun like this in Celtic times, or even earlier. Today the tidal stretch of the river has its length measured from Teddington Lock to the sea at the estuary mouth. The estuary provides both shelter from storms and also a funnel inviting invasion from the east; Danes and Vikings came spreading terror and the French were expected although they did not arrive. None of them could do it today – there are too many obstructions, the most modern being the tide-busters of the Thames Barrier at Woolwich. It is these same tides that made London the capital city of a vast and wealthy commercial empire, with ships returning from afar loaded with cargoes both exotic and prosaic. Upon the banks great wharves were set and lightermen, powered only by the forces of the tidal surge, sped hither and thither dividing the goods into smaller and smaller packets. Now the old Docklands are either wasted or are rising anew in modern buildings, and a fresh challenge to open up the riverside has been set. The Thames Path is part of that task and therefore part of London's cyclical metamorphosis.

Once called Thistleworth, the old village of Isleworth sits prettily by the river cramped by trees, water and parkland. The riverside of Syon Park is the last remaining stretch of natural tidal frontage on this part of the Thames and has been declared a Site of Special Scientific Interest. Its unique quality has caused the Thames Path to divert inland through the parkland closer to Syon House, the southern seat of the Dukes of Northumberland. Anyone familiar with the town of Alnwick will recognize the famous lion symbol of the Northumberlands with its distinctive ramrod-straight tail. The lion is evident here, too, atop the square,

Kew Gardens, London

Opposite Kew Palace the Thames is divided by Brentford Ait until just before Kew Bridge. The Thames Path runs along the full length of the outer wall of the Royal Botanic Gardens, which are well worth a detour. Kew Gardens are internationally famous for their plant and tree collections and contain buildings of national repute, such as the Orangery, Kew Palace and the mighty glasshouses. Here, work can be seen on the new Banks building and lake.

forceful house in its water meadow enhanced by Capability Brown. This leonine adornment originally stood in Northumberland Avenue in London and was brought by barge upriver from Charing Cross Pier.

In 1553, Lady Jane Grey was rowed downriver from Syon House, where her father-in-law, the Duke of Northumberland, was plotting to have her crowned queen. She reigned for a mere nine days before she and the ambitious Duke were imprisoned and beheaded the following year. Henry VIII's bloated corpse rested here briefly on its journey upstream and was attacked by rats before setting off for burial at Windsor.

The ford over the River Brent has long since been replaced by a bridge, and the river has been combined with the Grand Union Canal which enters the Thames at this point. Anyone wishing to walk north can turn off the Thames Path here and take the canal towpath to the Midlands. An old plaque on the bridge warned that any person wilfully injuring it would be kept in penal servitude for life.

Battles have been fought here: in 1016 against the Danes; in 1642 when Prince Rupert routed the Roundheads; and in the 1960s when good planning was defeated by the erection of massive tower blocks. Two unusual museums are hidden away near the riverside – the Living Steam Museum, with real steam engines, and the Musical Museum in St George's Church, which has a diverse collection of interesting and unusual instruments. Brentford and the canal provide the opportunity to create an exciting new footbridge for the Thames Path and a short cut through the Brentford Dock development.

Kew Gardens and Kew Green

On the southern bank the Thames Path strides out from Richmond Bridge past the tidal lock, Old Deer Park and Kew Observatory, with hardly a riverside intrusion before reaching the long wall of the Royal Botanic Gardens at Kew. The tall trees of the arboretum and the spike of the Chinese pagoda peep over the top of the wall and tempt further investigation. Who could resist visiting this green forest so close to the heart of the city? Not all that long ago the entrance fee to the gardens was one old penny, making them one of London's greatest bargains.

From the end of the eighteenth century until Victorian times these were the private gardens of the royal palace of Kew used by George III and Queen Charlotte. Kew Palace was built to a Dutch design (it was originally called the Dutch House) in 1631 by a rich merchant and in 1802 housed the royal couple's 15 children. Hidden away today inside Kew are some of the world's most wonderful plant drawings

Chiswick House, London

In its western approaches London still has time for green space and is not a solid conurbation of brick, steel and concrete. Chiswick House (built in 1725), although surrounded by domestic twentieth-century architecture, is a unique compliment to Palladio made by Lord Burlington and was designed after the style of Villa Capra in Italy. It was the popularization of this style by John Nash and others that has given us the glorious legacy of Regency buildings in Britain.

painted on expeditions all over the globe, and some are of species that were never found again. There are also the matchless dried herb and pressed flower collections.

Outside, in the 121-hectare (300-acre) parkland, is the 49.6 m (163-ft) high pagoda designed by Sir William Chambers in 1762 for George III's mother, the Dowager Princess of Wales, who founded Kew Gardens.

Kew's most splendid building must be the 1848 glass Palm House, designed by Decimus Burton before the arrival of the Crystal Palace. The Thames Path follows the riverside and Kew Gardens can be entered from it. The trees and plants are a sheer delight in any season, despite the ravages visited upon the place by the 1987 hurricane. On a sadder note, Edith Holden, author of *The Country Diary of an Edwardian Lady*, was drowned at Kew while hanging over the river to reach some horse chestnut buds.

Kew Green, standing outside the main gateway to the Royal Botanic Gardens, is an urban village green within the bustle of the South Circular Road but lined with well-preserved listed buildings of Georgian stock. Cricket is played here as if in the deepest countryside and St Anne's Church, containing the tombs of the eighteenth-century painters Thomas Gainsborough and John Zoffany, completes the manorial atmosphere.

The Thames Path from Chiswick

From Chiswick and Mortlake to the centre of London and beyond to Docklands, the river is wholly urban in character. This is not an oppressive quality, however, because nature still retains a grip on the environment at the water's edge and, especially along the Thames Path, trees and bushes grow thickly, giving a home to insects and birds. In these western approaches to Westminster the path is almost a park stretched out in a long line. It has even been imaginatively suggested that London's riversides should be revamped and made into the world's first wholly urban National Park.

Thames Path walkers share problems at Mortlake with unwary motorists who park outside the riverside pubs, little knowing the path is completely covered at high tide! Mortlake has some interesting waterfront housing and hides the site of England's first tapestry factory, which operated during the seventeenth century.

The Thames Path winds lazily through old village settlements such as Barnes, Hammersmith, Fulham and Putney towards Chelsea. Although wholly enmeshed in London brick they all retain some of the village atmosphere about them hidden at their centres.

Barnes surprises because of its leafy common, the weird and wonderful Harrods Depository building by the river and the ambitious plans to turn Barn Elms waterworks into a massive conservation area. This is a splendid idea financed by a planning gain deal. It will completely reshape the square water body into an intricate network of naturalistic lagoons of varying depths and feeding levels for resident and migrant birds. One of its most interesting ideas will be a tidal lagoon with a water level linked to the rise and fall of the Thames. There will be an interpretation centre named in memory of the naturalist Sir Peter Scott and the Thames Path will form its riverside boundary.

Over Hammersmith Bridge and beyond

The path crosses over the river to Hammersmith on one of the most remarkable of all the Thames bridges. Hammersmith Bridge hides a wealth of architectural details and was built in 1887 by Sir Joseph Bazalgette, whose municipal works are such a feature of the tidal Thames.

A little way downstream, Putney is known for its Common but less so for the last resting place of the literary Mrs Tiggywinkle, the hedgehog created by Beatrix Potter. The real hedgehog lived and died in Putney and her diminutive grave lies by the garden wall of a house near Earl's Court Underground station. The riverside landscape is better known for its boat houses and rowing clubs and forms the focus for London's rowing fraternity. The Thames Path's route is lined solid one Saturday in spring each year for that madcap sprint known as the Oxford and Cambridge Boat Race, which begins by Putney Bridge and ends at Mortlake.

Chelsea's riverside is both distinguished and loosely anchored. The blue plaques of Chelsea Embankment and Cheyne Walk reveal the hidden former haunts of painters James Whistler, Dante Gabriel Rossetti and J M W Turner, writers Leigh Hunt, Thomas Carlyle, George Eliot, Henry James and Hilaire Belloc, and the engineer Isambard Kingdom Brunel. Bazalgette constructed the Chelsea Embankment (1847) and modified the Albert Bridge. Chelsea hides Crosby Hall, an early example of a half-timbered mobile home, which was erected in Bishopsgate in 1466, somehow survived the Great Fire of London of 1666 and was re-erected in Chelsea in 1910. Cheyne Walk (still one of London's most select addresses) is graced by ranks of proud houseboats on its riverside.

Chelsea has a secret passageway built under the Thames between Cremorne Pier and St Mary's Church, Battersea, but it is officially blocked up. The Chelsea Flower Show, held each May, is not exactly secret but the Physic Garden has been well hidden by the Society of Apothecaries since 1673. Its owner, Sir Hans Sloane, handed over the freehold in 1722 and within its soil were grown the very first Indian cotton seeds that were exported to Carolina in North America in 1732 – the start of an eventful slice of history for America and Africa. One can only wonder what might have happened if the gardener at Chelsea had accidentally pulled up the plants as weeds in 1731.

The most powerful elements in the built-up landscape of Chelsea and Battersea were power stations. Lots Road, Fulham and the indomitable Battersea Power Station had chimneys that stabbed the sky like columns from colossal Greek temple ruins. It is hard to conceive that Battersea was also the place, a century earlier, where J M W Turner patiently waited to capture the perfect setting sun on canvas. It is even more incongruous to think of Colonel Blood lurking in the reed beds here in 1671 ready to shoot Charles II as he came down to swim in the river.

Battersea, once famous for its asparagus beds, now has its dogs' home and the incomparable majesty of its defunct power station. St Mary's Church, where Turner sat by the vestry window, is an ancient sacred site and it was near here that the Celtic Battersea Shield was retrieved. William Blake, the English poet, mystic and artist, was married in this riverside church to Catherine Butcher in 1782. The present structure dates from 1777 but is dwarfed by Sir Giles Gilbert Scott's 102-m (335-ft)

high Battersea Power Station, built in 1936. The power station still stands, sadly minus its roof and all of its interior. An adventurous cantilevered section of Thames Path should have added to the excitement at the riverside if redevelopment had proceeded as planned. Few realize that nearby Battersea Park was constructed from waste material dug up during the construction of the Royal Victoria Docks and, indeed, opened by the royal Victoria in 1858.

Westminster and the Embankment

Leaving behind the power stations for the power corridors, the eminence of Barry and Pugin's Houses of Parliament has been marred by the 1963 Swinging London landmark of the Millbank Tower, which casts a real shadow over the nearby Tate Gallery. Sir Henry Tate, the sugar magnate, gave his private collection of 65 British paintings and £80,000 to have the gallery erected in 1897. Art has arisen out of misery because the Tate is built over the site of the Millbank Penitentiary, London's largest prison until its closure in 1890.

Victoria Tower Gardens are green and succulent amidst the increasing bustle of traffic, and contain the renowned 1895 sculpture of the Burghers of Calais by the French sculptor Auguste Rodin. In the river near here someone may yet find the Great Seal of England that James II dropped, or threw away, when fleeing the kingdom on 11 December 1688 during the Glorious Revolution.

This potential for emergency exits also played an important role in the defensive design of the Houses of Parliament after the Duke of Wellington had a close shave with some rioters in 1832 during the passage of the Reform Bill. The Old Palace of Edward the Confessor was burnt down in 1834 but the adjacent Westminster Hall, started by William Rufus in 1097 and rebuilt by Richard II in 1399, is now incorporated in the Houses of Parliament. The new building took 12 years to complete and was opened in 1852. It was hit by 14 bombs during the Second World War and partly rebuilt between 1948–50. The bell, Big Ben, in the world-famous St Stephen's clock tower, is named after Sir Benjamin Hall, the first Commissioner of Works. Big Ben weighs 14 tonnes (14 tons) and was cast in Mears Foundry, Whitechapel Road, in 1858. It first rang on 31 May 1859. Big Ben replaced an equally large bell cast in 1856 near Stockton-on-Tees which was taken away in disgrace and smashed up because it didn't sound right. The clock face is 7.010 m (23 ft) across but

The Boat Race, Putney

The universities of Oxford and Cambridge come to London once a year to take part in the British sporting institution known as the Varsity Boat Race. Here on the second Saturday before Easter the crews of Oxford and Cambridge row, as if their lives depended upon it, between the University Stone, Putney and Mortlake Bridge. The race has been rowed here since 1845 and a number of collisions, sinkings and other mishaps have enlivened the event for spectators if not the crews.

not as big as the clock on the nearby Shell-Mex House, which is 7.018 m (25 ft 3 in) wide and is the largest in Britain; it is nicknamed Big Benzine.

Before 1882, when the Royal Courts of Justice were commissioned, judgment and trial took place in Westminster Hall and judges were summoned by Edward I's ancient bell, Great Tom, which stood at the spot now occupied by Big Ben.

The Thames Path passes between the Houses of Parliament and Westminster Abbey and the whole history of the power of the Establishment. However, the power of Church and State was not as strong as the Great Stink of 1858. The smell of raw sewage from the river, which overcame sittings of Parliament (after the mass replacement of earth closets by the new water-swilling lavatories), was an environmental hazard that even the hanging of sheets soaked in chloride of lime at the windows of Westminster could not counter. Bazalgette was commissioned to build the Victoria Embankment between 1863 and 1870 not only to divert the offensive sewage downstream but also to carry the new District Line Underground. Westminster Abbey was originally built on an island in the Thames and mudflats covered the land where the Houses of Parliament now stand. It is difficult to imagine this busy part of London today as estuarine marshland.

Once past the Houses of Parliament and Westminster Bridge, the Thames Path runs along the Embankment. This stretch of road lined with London plane trees is a fine example of Victorian civil engineering and features interesting *objets d'art* along its length. Cleopatra's Needle (dating from about 1500 BC), an Egyptian granite column erected by Thothmes III and given to Britain in 1819 by a grateful Mohammed Ali is one such example. It journeyed here in 1878 in a specially designed cylindrical boat that was abandoned in a storm and nearly sank in the Bay of Biscay. Hidden beneath it for future generations to discover are a variety of articles, including four Bibles in different languages, a set of coins, some newspapers, a copy of Bradshaw's *Railway Guide* and photographs of 12 of the most attractive Englishwomen of the day.

Sir Joseph Bazalgette was knighted for his engineering work and he has a plaque on the Embankment, but his lasting hidden memorial is the 2092 km (1300 miles) of sewers beneath London which drained into massive new sewage plants downstream at Beckton and Crossness. Today it is very easy to forget that cholera was almost endemic in London and that in 1849 infected water supplies killed 14,000 people. Even royalty could not escape disease, and Queen Victoria's beloved consort, Prince Albert, died of typhoid.

The Houses of Parliament, Westminster

Barry and Pugin's masterpiece, the Houses of Parliament, were built in mock medieval style and stand firm and ruler straight along the embanked Thames. Here the riverside terrace is revealed, where MPs and peers entertain and enjoy the view of the now mighty river. In the distance lie Lambeth Bridge and the lush green trees of Victoria Tower Gardens.

The Thames Path in Central London is a favourite promenade for office workers, commuters and theatre-goers, especially on the South Bank which it shares with the Shell Centre, County Hall (once the home of the Greater London Council, now abolished), the Royal Festival Hall, the National Film Theatre and the National Theatre. At night the riverside is awash with lights and entertainment, and the vast curve of the Thames as it sweeps majestically downriver glows with floodlit buildings set on both banks, providing a magnificent sight.

At the time of writing, only parts of the Thames Path are available through Central London and other sections, particularly in the City and Docklands, will have to await redevelopment. The line of the path, however, has been secured in all the necessary borough council plans for the future and should be completed by 2010.

The City of London

There is plenty of interest to offer the visitor in the City, with modern buildings, medieval architectural gems and old alleyways crammed into the square mile of the old Roman town plan, which comprised the original London. Gateways have marked the entrances to the City since Roman times, although seven of the original eight have now vanished forever, leaving just their names behind to serve as memorials – Aldgate, Bishopsgate, Ludgate, Aldersgate, Moorgate, Cripplegate and Newgate (also the site of the notorious prison). Temple Bar, built by Sir Christopher Wren in 1672, is the only one that remains standing, although not in London – it was moved stone by stone to Theobalds' Park in Hertfordshire in 1878 after it became a traffic hazard.

In 1582, the centre of the City of London was at Cornhill, between Bishopsgate and Leadenhall Street. A water conduit there became known as The Standard, and from it all of the standard distances to other towns were measured.

The City is rich with history and fascinating buildings, and there are many excellent and detailed guide books available that will be invaluable to walkers wishing to stray off the Thames Path to go exploring. The places mentioned here are mere tips of a giant historic iceberg.

The church of the City is St Lawrence Jewry, which dates from the twelfth century. It was twice destroyed by fire, and its modern weathervane is a grid iron to remind us of the manner of poor St Lawrence's martyrdom. Another City church, St Mary

Big Ben, Westminster

Strictly speaking, Big Ben is just a great bell, although everyone calls the bell tower in which it is housed by the same name – it should really be called St Stephen's Tower. Behind Big Ben lies Westminster Abbey, built on the former compact gravel of Thorney Isle when hereabouts was all river and marsh, and behind that the tall red brick tower of the Anglican abbey's Roman Catholic counterpart, Westminster Cathedral.

King's Reach, London

The stretch of the river between Blackfriars Bridge and Waterloo Bridge is called King's Reach. Moored to the Embankment, which runs along the northern shore all the way to Westminster Bridge, are historic ships such as the *Wellington* and *Chrysanthemum*. On the farther shore are the concrete buildings of the National Theatre, Royal Festival Hall and the Shell Centre, whilst Hungerford Railway Bridge takes the railway into Charing Cross Station. The green trees in the middle distance belong to the airy legal courtyards of The Temple. The site was formerly occupied by the heretic Order of Knights Templar from 1160 to 1308, but now provides England and Wales with its barristers. Ludgate Circus, Fleet Street and St Bride's Church occupy the foreground.

Aldermanbury, which was built by Wren in 1700, was dismantled in 1946 and re-erected in Fulton, Missouri, USA as a tribute to Sir Winston Churchill. In this transplanted church Churchill first uttered the words 'The Iron Curtain' to describe the Communist bloc.

It is all the more interesting that, since the melting down of the symbol of Communist ideology, the 'invisible curtain' of the boundary of the City of London (within which run its peculiar customs, rights, privileges, police force and market institutions) is still largely in existence. The Corporation of the City of London owed most of its nineteenth-century wealth to the fact that it imposed a tax on all shipments (especially of coal) passing through its control (mostly along the Thames). This power had some unusual spin-offs and the preservation of both Epping Forest in Essex and Burnham Beeches in Buckinghamshire is due to the actions of the Corporation in the nineteenth century.

The Roman walls on which the City boundary is based can still be seen in parts, and plaques mark other places where the City wall once stood. Redevelopment constantly brings to light fresh evidence of London's hidden archaeological treasures. It has also reduced the City's resident population: in 1801 it was 120,000 but by 1951 it was a mere 5000.

The Old Bailey

Sandwiched conveniently between State and City is the legal part of London, handily placed to serve two masters. The top echelon of legal affairs below the House of Lords is handled by the Royal Courts of Justice in the Strand, and nearby are the Inns of Court at Temple. The Old Bailey on Newgate Street is the Central Criminal Court of London and home of infamous trials and courtroom dramas. It is built over the site of the equally infamous Newgate Prison, which took over the role of official place of execution from Tyburn in 1783. The last public execution here was of Michael Barrett, on 26 May 1868, who was convicted of trying to blow up the Middlesex House of Detention, although private executions continued until 1901. The architect E W Mountford designed the existing building in 1902 with its copper dome; the statue of Justice by F W Pomeroy is cast in bronze. The statue

The Old Bailey and St Paul's Cathedral, The City

St Paul's Cathedral has been cruelly hemmed in by uninspired office blocks and deserves a little space in which to breathe, but nowhere in London can any office executive view Justice in the eye quite like this, with St Paul's as a backcloth. F W Pomeroy's famous statue of the bronzed avenger, with her scales and double-edged sword, stands atop the Old Bailey and is usually hidden from sight by encroaching buildings.

strangely echoes that medieval instrument of punitive discipline, the pillory, which was last used in Britain on this site on 24 June 1830 when a Mr Bossy was pilloried for one hour for perjury.

St Paul's Cathedral

One of Britain's most famous landmarks and the crowning achievement of Sir Christopher Wren's inspired career, St Paul's Cathedral is visited by hundreds of thousands of people each year. Sadly it does not command the same visual prominence on the London skyline as it did 40 years ago: all around it are high-rise towers which lack the grace of St Paul's 111-m (365-ft) high dome. What Wren would have thought of the architectural subjugation of his masterpiece is hard to imagine.

The first known church to stand on this spot was erected by St Ethelbert, King of Kent, in 604. It is not recorded whether this was a former pagan site although St Paul's is aligned with other churches on earlier sacred sites, which may indicate pre-Christian origins.

The Great Fire of London in 1666 destroyed the old Norman cathedral and Wren constructed the one we know today between 1675 and 1710 out of fashionable Portland stone. The pile of rubble from the old cathedral was dumped into a mound 100.5 m (330 ft) long and 54.8 m (180 ft) wide, which was known as Whitechapel Mount until 1808 when the Corporation of London shifted it. Wren, a professor of astronomy before he became an architect, rebuilt more than 50 churches after the Great Fire, including the Cockney's church of St Mary-le-Bow in Cheapside. Appropriately, he is buried in St Paul's.

The Monument and London Bridge

London abounds in monuments and the riverside is cluttered with them, but there is only one Monument. It is 61.5 m (202 ft) high and stands exactly 61.5 m (202 ft) from the shop in Pudding Lane where the Great Fire of London started in 1666. Yet another of Sir Christopher Wren's contributions to London during the 1670s, the Monument is alleged to be the tallest free-standing hollow stone column in the world. The Great Fire killed only 11 people but it destroyed 13,000 medieval houses and wiped out the Elizabethan City of London in 4 days. It followed the Great

The Monument, The City

Sir Christopher Wren constructed this hollow pillar between 1671–7 to commemorate the Great Fire of London of 1666. It is said to be the tallest stone column in the world. A most unusual view of the surrounding cityscape can be obtained from the platform, but it is not as bizarre as this view of the Monument as we peer down its gilded throat.

Plague of 1665, which killed 7000 people on one September day alone. The fire burnt out the festering slums and the rats, carriers of the killer disease, but it also took with it 87 churches and nearly every half-timbered building. Samuel Pepys, watching from the church of All Hallows by the Tower, recorded the disaster in graphic detail in his diary, although his secret shorthand was not deciphered until 1825. The Monument also marked the northern end of the original London Bridge.

The site of London Bridge is very old and probably Roman, but certainly Saxon, although stone was not used before the London Bridge of 1176, which survived until 1831. This was the only bridge across the Thames in London until 1749.

Infamous for its displays of rotting traitors' heads on pikestaffs, the old stone bridge also acted as a partial tidal barrage and slowed the Thames sufficiently for it to freeze over and host the great Frost Fairs of 1564-5, 1683–4, 1715-6, 1739-40 and 1813-14, when oxen were roasted and bulls baited. The old London Bridge was a town in itself, jutting out proudly over the Thames with houses, shops and a church jettied on to the multi-arched bridgework. An enterprising Dutchman even had a waterwheel installed in one arch and drew power from the current to pump water. Between 1831 and 1832 John Rennie built a classical granite bridge to replace it, which stood until 1968 when the demands of the motor car proved too much. Then the incredible happened – the McCulloch Corporation of USA paid $2,460,000 to buy the 10,246 pieces of stonework and had it re-erected across Lake Havasu, Arizona, on 9 October 1971.

Despite being celebrated in song and as part of the folk lore of national culture, the modern London Bridge, built by Mott, Hay and Anderson between 1967 and 1972, is fairly plain. The Thames Path crosses this bridge, and all the others, should any walkers wish to make a comparative study of London's bridges.

The Tower of London

Billingsgate, London's former fish market, and Custom House (which is another of the buildings rebuilt by Sir Christopher Wren after the Great Fire) have long stood between London Bridge and the Tower of London. The Tower, like St Paul's, is one of Britain's best-loved tourist attractions and, even for those unprepared for the high entrance fees, boasts an excellent stretch of Thames Path that runs between it and the river. This place has all the ingredients of every child's ideal aggression-releasing play – cannons, mortars, a castle with a blood-soaked history and a real battleship

The Monument, The City

Only the pigeons regularly see London from this viewpoint, although even the birds probably have difficulty obtaining a purchase on the Monument's gilded top piece. For human beings without the ability to fly the bad news is that there are 311 steps up to the viewing platform. As well as commemorating the Great Fire of London the Monument also marks the position of the entrance to the old London Bridge on the City side of the river.

Tower Bridge and the Upper Pool, The City

On a misty day, with the sunlight breaking through, the river takes on an older feel, remembering perhaps the old pea-souper smogs or the smoke from the blitzed Docklands. Before 1831, when Charles Rennie rebuilt London Bridge, the river here would have been crowded with shipping and penned in by the impassable barrier of the ancient bridge. Here on the river's edge is old Billingsgate Market and the Custom House. Billingsgate was built by Sir Horace Jones in 1875, although a free fish market was established here in 1699. The Custom House dates from 1813–25; it is built in yellow brick and fringed by trees at the water's edge. A custom house has been here since 870. HMS *Belfast* is moored permanently opposite the Tower of London as an outpost of the Imperial War Museum and Tower Bridge guards the river in Gothic splendour.

moored on the opposite bank of the Thames. The riverside entry into the military stronghold, through the chilling Traitors' Gate, lies beneath the Thames Path and is best seen from one of the excellent tourist river boats that motor up and down the Thames. This portal was one of the many later additions that make up the Tower as we know it today.

Over the centuries, since a temporary fort was first built here in around 1066 and buildings were erected piecemeal whenever they were needed, the Tower has been a palace, prison, place of execution, mint, museum, observatory and zoo, and even contains London's oldest church, St John's Chapel. Public executions took place on Tower Green (private ones involved secret garrotings inside), and many famous names met their end here.

The Crown Jewels used to be kept in Westminster Abbey until stolen by Richard Podicote in the fourteenth century. Podicote was caught, flayed alive and the jewels kept in the Tower thereafter. The crown was 'borrowed' as a stunt by Colonel Blood on 9 May 1671 but his fate was very different – when he was caught he managed to charm Charles II into giving him a healthy pension and estates in Ireland. The Tower is also famous for its Beefeaters, who guard it in their scarlet coats, and the ravens who wear glossy black ones.

The ravens have their wings clipped every three months by the Raven Master to ensure they do not fly away and allow a curse to strike Britain. This superstition may be linked to the legend of the burial of Bran the Blessed's head under the White Hill of London, which was described in the *Mabinogion*, the fourteenth-century Welsh epic that is in turn based on a much older story. The legend of Bran's head stated that, as long as its location was not disclosed, England would be safe from invasion. The same is said of the ravens (despite their inability to fly away!) and Charles II was alleged to have introduced them to the Tower of London for that very reason. Bran was the Celtic word for raven.

The cult of the head (usually severed) is characteristically Celtic. The head was believed to be the home of the soul and capable of divinity. It is likely, therefore, that the ravens are living metaphors of this Celtic belief. It also seems possible that the White Tower of William the Conqueror (1078) was built over the ancient holy site known as the White Hill or White Mount. Perhaps William himself was mindful of the legend of Bran's head and chose this place for the Tower of London because of its powerful associations as a protective national talisman.

Tower Bridge and the Tower of London, The City

Tower Bridge is one of the most fantastic designs of any bridge anywhere in the world, and its Gothic style of 1894 outshines all modern architectural competitors. Indeed, the design was chosen as the result of a competition. The Tower of London now stands quietly alongside on the City bank, although its history has been far from peaceful. A section of the Thames Path runs in front of it.

Tower Bridge and the Pool of London

Even though the Tower of London is well furnished with the stuff of myths, mystery and legend, the landscape of the Pool of London is dominated by the power and might of Tower Bridge. Hidden inside this remarkable bridge are all manner of mechanical contraptions and the still-functioning bascule lifting gear. Opened on 30 June 1894, it was the million-pound marvel of its age. When the Pool of London was a busy place, the steam-operated drawbridge pistons were in frequent use and lattice footbridges between the twin Gothic towers allowed an uninterrupted pedestrian passageway. These walkways were originally covered and gloomy but after renovation they now provide one of the most stimulating public views of the River Thames and London. Unfortunately, the bridge rarely opens now, but in 1952 it opened before the traffic was stopped, and a bus had to hop the considerable gap over the middle of the river. It seems that even machinery capable of raising two 1000-tonne (1000-ton) bascules in two minutes goes wrong sometimes.

Despite the chance to take the free Thames Path route across the river here at road level, walkers should not miss the opportunity to pay a small fee and ascend the higher walkway – they will not be disappointed. They will be able to gaze upstream at HMS *Belfast*, the largest British cruiser of the Second World War, moored and used as a museum, while downstream they will see St Katharine's Dock, with its flotilla of interesting and ancient boats, such as a red and white striped Light Vessel and Scott of the Antarctic's ship RRS *Discovery*. On the Southwark bank is the site of the Clink, which has given its name to prisons everywhere, and the Globe, Swan and Rose Theatres which act as reminders of Shakespeare's London. Although very little remains of these wooden buildings, elements of them keep emerging as redevelopment proceeds alongside the Thames Path. Those fragments strike a deep chord in the national cultural psyche because of the vital importance these early tiered theatres-in-the-round played in the development of the theatrical arts and English literature worldwide.

Docklands and the Isle of Dogs

The river below Tower Bridge is still thickly crowded with decaying piers, jetties, wharves and the dockside paraphernalia of waterborne transportation and transhipment. There are a few lighters and barges on the Thames, but on the whole the scene is one of redundancy and mutation. This is in stark contrast to the enormity of London's former trade and the Lowryesque picture of frantic human and industrial activity in and around the Port of London. This was once the bustling landscape of the greatest port in the world.

The Thames Path has to complete its most difficult sections here because the riversides have never developed towpaths or embankments for communication. The banks were crammed solid with chaotically clogged wharves, bonded wharves, warehouses, steps and the custom or legal quays where dutiable goods had to be handled. Passageways and alleys down which Charles Dickens' characters, such as Fagin and Bill Sykes, might have hurried on their nefarious business, led off at right angles to the river to meet narrow cobbled roads like Wapping High Street which are linked landward to further areas of warehousing. Until the riverside path is completed it is along these streets that the route of the Thames Path will run. They are less murderously hazardous now than in the days of Jack the Ripper or the lethal pea-soupers which killed thousands of Londoners (mostly through lung disease but occasionally – when the smogs were at their thickest – by people falling in the river). The views which have now opened up following the clearances of old buildings are both confusing and amazing to the people who have lived here all their lives.

Docklands was a place driven by animal and human muscle, the winds, tides and, later, steam. To fuel these demands and similar ones elsewhere in the capital a massive trade in hay for horses and coal for industry and domestic fires developed. Hay came on 'stackies', which were special sail barges, from the marshes of Kent and Essex (and then went back there as manure for the fruit farms), and coal came in colliers from Newcastle. With the coal came Geordies and North-Easterners such as Captain Cook, from Whitby, on collier ships built from wood. The Prospect of Whitby pub at Wapping (frequented in their respective days by Samuel Pepys, Charles Dickens, James Whistler and J M W Turner, among others) celebrates one such ship, named the *Prospect*, which was registered at Whitby. Cook's ship the *Endeavour*, in which he explored the Pacific Ocean, was also a converted collier.

In large measure, the wealth of London was founded on humble coal. In 1861 nearly 3.5 million tonnes (3.5 million tons) of coal were delivered into London by sea on 2717 ships. With it came 21,600 sailors, some no doubt later employed on 'flatties', which were boats built to be low in the water so they could pass under the Thames bridges on their way to fuel the power stations and gas works upstream. Sailors lived in the 'sailor towns', although as many as one third of them had no homes at all and were easy prey to pimps (known as crimpers) in a landscape where every fifth house was a pub or brothel.

The growth and decline of the Docks

It was different on the river, where lightermen steered their tide-driven barges through the mass of shipping, using skills now almost lost forever. In 1794 there were 3663 ships unloading goods in London, and the City merchants were unable to keep track of everything, with much of it being pilfered by scuffle hunters, mudlarks and river pirates. Docks were the only answer and in 1802 the West India Docks were opened on the Isle of Dogs. This was once a green field with a name derived from the Dutch engineers who drained the marshland with *dijks* (ditches). In 1805 the London Docks opened in Wapping and then Blackwall a year later. The Surrey Commercial Docks opened through an accident, when a scheme to dig a canal from London to Kent only got as far as Peckham. It was joined up with the Greenland (whale products) Dock and three other companies. It covered a massive area in grain and timber imports and was famous for its 'deal porters', who balanced enormous quantities of sawn timber on their shoulders.

One of the last docks to open (in 1828), was St Katharine's, which can be observed so well from Tower Bridge. To make way for it a hospital was knocked down and 11,300 people evicted from their homes. More docks were opened in the 1850s –

The City of London

The wealth that created the City of London came from a multitude of sources, but wool and coal perhaps stand out historically as the main providers of tax or profit until more recent times. Banking, insurance and the sterile electronic dealing in money today mean that the City financiers no longer look towards the river even though their towers and offices reach ever higher to overlook each other.

BUTLERS WHARF

Armada Tudor

Greenwich, London

The mast tops of the tea clipper the *Cutty Sark*, marooned for ever in dry dock at Greenwich Pier, intrude into Greenwich's historic heartland. Greenwich Old Royal Observatory can be seen amongst the trees in Greenwich Park, through which the 0 degrees line of longitude passes and where Greenwich Mean Time began in 1833. The park was commissioned by Charles II and laid out by Le Nôtre, the designer of Versailles. The original observatory was built for the first Astronomer Royal by Sir Christopher Wren. Down by the riverside comparison should be drawn between Sir Francis Chichester's yacht *Gipsy Moth IV*, in which he made his solo circumnavigation of the world, and the *Cutty Sark*. Greenwich's maritime connections are enriched by Wren's baroque Royal Naval College, completed in 1705, and the National Maritime Museum.

Victoria Docks in 1855, Millwall in 1864 and the South West India Dock in 1870 – but the decline was imminent. In 1866, Tilbury Docks, closer to the Thames estuary, opened and trade began its inexorable drift downstream.

In 1909 the commercial chaos on the river was interfering with good business and so the Port of London Authority was created. It opened the modern George V Dock in 1921 but saw the Nazi bombers of 1940 destroy many of its improvements. All of the timber wharves caught fire, the sugar warehouses turned to burning treacle which spread on to the water and provided a beacon for the returning Luftwaffe, and 430 Docklands residents died on the night of 7 September 1940.

The docks never returned to prominence and steadily declined through the 1960s and 1970s. In 1981 the last great docks, known collectively as the Royals, closed and the London Docklands Development Corporation was formed.

Despite the architectural and business transformation in the 1980s and 1990s, there are still hidden corners and reminders of the old river life. Some unbombed pubs cling to their ancient sites, such as the Angel, Town of Ramsgate, Mayflower, Grapes and the aforementioned Prospect of Whitby, but old Docklands only exists in the imagination and Dickensian slivers of Bermondsey, Millwall and Wapping. Now the towering peak of Canary Wharf rises high above new architectural foothills riven by the sinuous path of the Docklands Light Railway.

The sugary, spicy smells of old Docklands will catch the noses of Londoners no more and remain hidden in the folk memories of East London forever.

Greenwich

South of the Isle of Dogs and east of Deptford is Greenwich, with what must surely be one of the most hidden places in London – the pedestrian tunnel that runs beneath the Thames and links Greenwich Pier on the south bank with Island Gardens on the Isle of Dogs on the north. It was built by the London County Council in 1902 and has been fun for children of all ages ever since. It now provides links with the Docklands Light Railway, the preserved tea clipper the *Cutty Sark* and the spot that Sir Christopher Wren thought showed off his work on the Royal Naval College to best advantage.

Greenwich, of course, is where time begins or, at least, began in 1833 when the first public time signal started operating at the Old Royal Observatory. Building upon this horological success in 1884, Greenwich was declared 0 degrees longitude

Canary Wharf, The Isle of Dogs

The Isle of Dogs is now being rapidly developed, amid much controversy, and is already busy changing the face of this part of London. Towering high above everything else stands Canary Wharf, London's tallest building by far, bringing the flavour of New York's skyscrapers to London's old docks. The Thames curves so much here that it is impossible from the river to tell on which bank Canary Wharf stands.

The Docklands, London

From marshland to the new centre of London's commercial activity in under two centuries? In 1799 an Act of Parliament authorized the West Indies Company to build a new dock here because the Port of London below the old London Bridge was clogged with shipping. The docks were completed in 1802 and the Millwall Docks added in 1864. With a monopoly of West Indian goods, particularly sugar, the docks prospered. In the twentieth century, containerization and Tilbury Docks (built for bigger ships and closer to the sea) condemned the Isle of Dogs to commercial death.

and given Greenwich Mean Time, in order to control standards in world time, at an international conference in Washington, USA. Greenwich Park, in which the observatory stands, was designed for Charles II by Le Nôtre, the creator of Versailles, who planned it sight unseen and didn't realize it was on a hill.

Henry VIII and his daughters Elizabeth and Mary were all born here at the Tudor mansion called The Palace of Placentia, and Mary II commissioned Wren to rebuild it as a home for disabled seamen. Completed in 1705, it was given over to the education of officers in 1873 when the seamen were awarded pensions instead. Queen's House, designed by Inigo Jones in 1619, is graciously placed next to Wren's contribution to splendid effect. Hidden beneath these Palladian and Baroque piles is allegedly the site of that famous puddle over which Sir Walter Raleigh spread his cloak so Elizabeth I wouldn't get her feet wet.

The *Cutty Sark* is in dry dock on the site of the Old Ship Tavern, which played host to some curious Victorian ritual eating on Whit Sundays. These were the Whitebait Dinners of the late nineteenth century, when herring and sprat fry were caught, fried and eaten, all within the hour. Members of Parliament became caught up in this Thames-side frivolity because it also marked the start of the summer recess. Ministers of the party in power dined at the Trafalgar Tavern while the Loyal Opposition went to the Old Ship.

The Thames Barrier at Woolwich

The official end (or starting point) of the Thames Path is the Thames Barrier Centre at Woolwich. The Barrier itself is a potent symbol of the Thames, although it represents the power of nature rather than the supremacy of technology. It was completed in October 1982 at a cost of £535 million after eight years of construction under the authority of the Greater London Council, and is one of a series of palliative, anti-flood measures in the estuary. A number of bad floods on the non-tidal river (including the devastating one of 1947) and surge tides downstream had concentrated minds on how to protect London's vulnerable population and Underground services. However, the experiences of the 1953 storm in the Thames Estuary and East Anglia, when over 300 people died, were particularly forceful arguments in favour of its construction. The Barrier is a sophisticated and daring piece of engineering with cowled piers supporting hidden gates and counterweights, each weighing 3700 tonnes (3700 tons) and resting on the river bed

The Thames Barrier, Woolwich

The Thames Barrier marks the end (or the beginning) of the Thames Path and the Visitor Centre on the southern bank acts as the ceremonial focus for everyone, whether they are at the start or finish of their journey. The Barrier can also form the dividing line between the river and the sea; here the massive power of the tide is being held back by the vertical gates, each of which normally repose flat on the river bed to allow shipping to pass by unhindered.

E
D
C
7
B
8
9

until needed. It is regularly tested and the North Sea weather is constantly monitored. In an emergency it takes 30 minutes to raise the gates into position.

Although the Thames Path reaches its climax here at Woolwich, the river itself rolls strong, wide and dark out towards the estuary mouth and the sea, pulled by the constant tides. London's commercial centre is also being pulled downstream by the equally constant demands of greater space and new technology. Added impetus to this expansion is being given by the East London Corridor Study and the Channel Tunnel rail link. The remaining precious estuarine marshes of the Thames are being closely examined for potential development sites. It would be encouraging to think that the lessons of the past could be reviewed so that nature and its remaining wild places are not swept away by this process. Thames Chase, East London's exciting new community forest, is being planted north of Rainham and Dagenham marshes and London should pay closer attention to its landward green places along its great river. The opportunity to create a better riverside that is accessible to everyone – tree-lined, emparked and entertaining but still active and attractive to those who live and work on it – should not be missed.

Much has already changed but the new Thames Path, which is the cloudy brown river's silver lining, is the link between it all from source to sea and the vital catalyst in a new vision for the river in the twenty-first century.